From Artisan's Son to Hamlet: The Life of August Schønemann, Comedy King of Norway

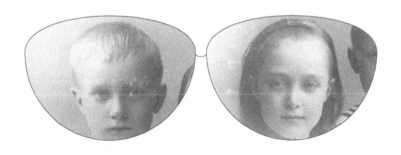

Snorre Smári Mathiesen

Published in the USA by
BearManor Media
1317 Edgewater Dr. #110
Orlando, FL 32804
www.BearManorMedia.com

Softcover Edition
ISBN-10:
ISBN-13: 979-8-88771-048-8

Printed in the United States of America

Dedicated to my Dad, Thomas. I am grateful that you encouraged my weird hobbies and projects, whether they involved cartooning or nearly-forgotten silent film stars. Miss you deeply.

Contents

Introduction 7

History of Norway – A Summary 11

1. Paperer Pettersen 17
2. Tormentors & Twist...27
3. *Charley's Aunt*...37
4. Fahlstrøm and Qværnstrøm.....................................43
5. «TIVOLI» of Christiania Tivoli 56
6. Futt..65
7. A Chaplinesque Kick in the Belly............................77
8. «Seven Roles Tonight»...86
9. Casino..97
10. Silver Screen Stunts...119
11. Fatherhood..134
12. Comedy King Meets Ex-Emperor 144
13. Without A Thread..158
14. Idol of the Gallery..170

Selected stage chronology 188

Filmography..198

Bibliography..199

About the Author 205

Index 206

Introduction

When one reads reviews of August Schønemann (born Pettersen) in Norwegian press – especially from 1915 forward – one thing remains clear above all else: August Schønemann possessed *star quality*. The little man with the expressive face was not only *funny*, he truly mesmerized the public from whatever stage he appeared on, with an endless variety of characters. The awe that he inspired not just among fans, but usually also theater critics, puts it beyond doubt that Schønemann could rival the great international comedy stage stars of the time, such as Al Jolson and Eddie Cantor. Although Schønemann's style, at times, bordered on the grotesque – his «tailor» character in the revue *Overalls* (1920) is one example of this, or the reluctant «lion tamer» (1923) – he could also, by numerous accounts, be remarkably subtle in his gestures onstage, depending on what fit best in a given scenario. According to some later accounts, Schønemann was even nicknamed «Norway's Charlie Chaplin», although yours truly has not been able to find any item from the comedian's own lifetime naming him as such (the accuracy of the epithet is debatable anyhow, as Chaplin, of course, became primarily famous for his Little Tramp character, whereas Schønemann made a career of transforming himself into dozens of comic figures. Furthermore, Schønemann became equally beloved for his performances of comic songs, as he did for his comic characters).

In contrast to the aforementioned international stars, Schønemann passed away tragically young, at a time when the possibilities of preserving his legacy were limited – and moreover, this was not something that anyone bothered to prioritize in little Norway. By comparison, it has been said that Al Jolson's stage charisma was never quite captured onscreen, which may be true; but through his many film appearances, we may, at least, get a *sense* of what an irresistible stage presence he must've been. August Schønemann is far worse off in this regard. Other than posters, reviews and photographs, *one* silent film and a few gramophone records are pretty much all that survive.

I have wished with this book to demonstrate and map out the significance of August Schønemann as a revue artist in Scandinavia during the early 20th century, and I hope to, perhaps, contribute to a «Schønemann rediscovery» of a kind. Also to readers outside of Norway, I believe his story deserves to be told, especially to anyone interested in revue and film history.

Originally, I had this book self-published (in Norwegian), through a self-publishing service called Kolofon in 2018. However, a few years later, the American publisher BearManor Media (who in 2017 published my book *Max Linder: Father of Film Comedy*[1]) showed interest in properly publishing this book, and so I had it translated to American, updated with several additions to make it more reader-friendly to non-Norwegian readers, along with new «discoveries» on Schønemann's life. In other words, although largely a translation of the Norwegian edition, quite a bit of additional research has been done for this American version, such as on the comedian's family background in Chapter 1. Furthermore, in the Norwegian version, I did a few silly factual errors which I have aimed to get corrected this time, such as the main shooting location of Schønemann's only film, as well as some details concerning the operation of the vast «amusement area» of Christiania Tivoli. In Chapter 14, I also provide new information regarding Schønemann's diagnosis at the time of his death.

Schønemann's personal scrapbook (stored at the Norwegian National Library, Oslo) – in which he between 1909 and 1915 collected reviews of nearly every one of his stage appearances, along with professional contracts and personal commentary in the margins – has served as an indispensable resource for this book. Many thanks to Pål Pande-Rolfsen, Schønemann's grandchild, for making me aware of the scrapbook.

Haakon B. Nielson's chapter on Schønemann, in his awesome (Norwegian) book *Revystjerner i 1920-årenes Kristiania* («Revue stars in 1920s Kristiania», J. W. Cappelen 1970) has also been of great help. There are a few times in the book when my own findings contradict Nielson's, mostly on minor things such as a few dates, etc, but sometimes also regarding more notable aspects, such as Schønemann's reported cause of death. I will point out these contradictions, but please understand that it is not my intention, in any way, to undermine Nielson's great work. I am in debt for research he did as far back as the 1960s.

After 1915, Schønemann essentially lost interest in writing down his stage appearances in the scrapbook (probably because they became too numerous to note at that point), so for the remaining decade of his life, I have primarily relied on my own findings in old newspapers and journals, stored in the archives of the Norwegian National Library, in addition to Nielson's overview.

For information on Schønemann's residences during his lifetime, geneaology, marriage details, etc., my most important resource (by far) has been various church books and other documents stored at the Norwegian «Digital Archive» (Digitalarkivet). For more sources, see Bibliography and Notes.

All photographs not part of my own collection are used with permission.

I will mostly refer to Schønemann as «August» – or August Jr., considering that his father carried the same name, August Pettersen – in the first four chapters or so, whereas it feels more apt to use «Schønemann» when writing of the years after he'd achieved fame.

I may also remind readers that I sometimes include relevant information in the Notes section, beyond merely naming sources.

–Snorre Smári Mathiesen

Notes:

1. A few points in my book *Max Linder: Father of Film Comedy* which I may take the opportunity to correct and/or clarify (it's the same publisher, after all):

    *   Charles Pathé was 31 years old in 1894, not 37.

    *   From what I now understand (thanks to Lisa Stein Haven's excellent biography on Max), Max visited Charlie Chaplin's studio as the latter was busy making *The Adventurer* (1917), not *The Immigrant* (1917).

    *   A few times in the book, I adopted a somewhat "ironic" tone (such as when reciting some of the plots in Max's films which may appear a bit hard to swallow to modern audiences), something I've since become more cautious about doing in non-fiction writing. My point was that, if one can "accept" certain dated story premises in context of the films and the time they were made, these films often still stand as quite good little comedies.

    I may also point out a semantic error on p. 67: when writing about the film *Max's Hat* (1913), I state that "It's in snippets such as this [film] that Max's appeal is most *glaring*" – but it would, of course, have been more accurate to use a word such as *striking* ("glaring" being a word with negative undertones, which was not my intention).

    Also, I did use the phrase "to say the least" a bit much in the book, to say the least. I've tried to avoid similar overuse of the phrase in *this* book.

History of Norway – A Summary

(To give better context to non-Norwegian readers.)

As one of three *Scandinavian countries* – the other two being Sweden and Denmark – Norway is located in Northern Europe, and constitutes a total area of 385,207 square kilometres, with a long eastern border to Sweden on one side and a vast coastline on the other. The upper parts of the country border to Finland and Russia. Famous for its beautiful fjords and other notable geographical sights, it is also known for being the country where Henrik Ibsen, Edvard Grieg, Edvard Munch and Sonja Henie came from, but the country has also nurtured other, less internationally known artists through its history.

Although the country's economy rose rapidly in the decades following World War II, and all the more so when oil was found by the North Sea in the 1970s, it has been widely claimed that Norway, for centuries, was one of the poorest of countries in Europe. Some historians have argued that Norway's poverty, relative to the rest of Europe, prior to the 1900s has been overblown in retrospect, but poverty was indeed rampant among much of the population, a huge majority being farmers until the early 20th century. Despite being considerably larger than Denmark in physical size, in terms of political power, Norway was considered the «little» Scandinavian country from the 1300s onwards.

Brief Timeline

The period in Norwegian history which, in retrospect, has become known as the «Viking Age», may not warrant much coverage here, as it remains widely infamous. Usually accepted by historians to have lasted between the early 800s and 1066, during this phase, groups of Norsemen (including the geographical areas of today's Sweden and Denmark, in addition to Norway) embarked on voyages throughout Europe and (to some degree) other continents, resulting in trading, colonization, and brutal, massive raiding and killing. However, it's perhaps worth noting that the «Viking» aspect of this period has tended to be exaggerated in later popular culture. Even during the so-called «Viking Age», most Norwegians led ordinary lives, feeding themselves mainly through farming.

It was, however, during this time that a larger portion of Norway was first united, through the king of Harald Fairhair (c. 850 – c. 932).

While the «Viking voyages» practically reached their end with the death of Norwegian king Harald Hardrada (during the famous Battle of Stamford Bridge in 1066), the following 1100s and 1200s have later come to be known as a Norwegian «Golden Age». During this time, the country was considered a great power in Europe. The first State Law of the country was issued in the 1270s.

Then came other times. The Black Plague of 1349-50 hit Norway particularly hard, and proved more devastating to the country's economy and political situation than Sweden and Denmark. Its royal family extinct by the late 1300s, Norway went into union with Sweden and Denmark, and then with Denmark alone from 1450. In the 1530s, the Norwegian state was formally abolished, and so for more than a century, Danish nobility ruled over both Denmark *and* Norway. The Danish king, elected by the Danish *Riksråd* (Councils), had limited power during this period.

However, in 1660, following a war with Sweden, the Danish king Frederic III succeeded in overthrowing the state power and established «absolute monarchy» in the country, securing supreme power over Denmark-Norway to himself and his royal successors.

Various, sometimes highly eccentric kings ruled over Denmark-Norway for the next 150 years, with Christian VII (1749-1808) being perhaps the most infamous one, as he suffered from severe mental illness. In 1784, yet another *coup d'état* took place in Denmark-Norway, although this time behind closed doors, as the son of Christian VII, Crown prince Frederic VI, managed to trick his father into signing a paper, which instantly made Frederic into *de facto* ruler of the country (although, out of context, this act may have seemed cruel by Frederic VI, a good case could be made that it gave his father some much-needed placidity).

In the early years of the Napoleonic wars, Denmark-Norway wished to remain neutral, preferring the role of war profiteers, but saw it necessary to join French side after Great Britain attacked Copenhagen in an attempt to acquire the country's military ships. Following the defeat of Napoleon (prior to his brief «comeback» in 1815), Denmark wound up having to give up Norway to Sweden. For the next 90 years, Norway was ruled by the Swedish king, but, unlike what had been the case during the centuries of Danish reign, the country was now allowed to form its own government and constitution.

Largely inspired by the American Constitution of 1776, and philosophical undercurrents in Europe of the time, the Norwegian Constitution of 1814 was regarded as highly modern in its day, even radical by some. The importance of (relative) freedom of speech was emphasized, in stark contrast to what had been the case during the years of absolute monarchy. However, in the name of nuance, it should, perhaps, be stressed that the Constitution also included clauses rife of prejudices, which will appear deeply problematic to modern eyes. Although Norway, with time, gained the reputation of being a «pioneering» country with regards to the introduction of various progressive ideas – of the Scandinavian countries, it was the first to give women full voting rights (1913) – this reputation has, perhaps, not always been entirely justified.

During the «Romantic Era» of the 1800s, writers, artists and composers sought to establish a Norwegian cultural «identity» in the country, after more than 400 years of Danish influence. «Forgotten» Norwegian folk music, myths, and fairytales served as inspiration in this regard. Meanwhile, power struggle developed between the Norwegian government and the Swedish monarch. In an attempt to secure the power of the government (and, in turn, further diminish the power of the king), parliamentarism was established in Norway in 1884.

By 1905, the Swedish-Norwegian union was repealed – not without some turbulence, although war was avoided in the end – making Norway into a completely independent state. The Danish prince Christian Frederic, later known as Haakon VII (d. 1957), was selected as new king, but the days of monarchs possessing actual political power in Norway were now a thing of the past – although Norway remains a «constitutional monarchy» to this day.

It's worth pointing out that Norway's capital city, Oslo, went under the name of *Christiania* from 1624 to 1924 – usually spelled **Kristiania** from the late 1800s – after the Danish king of Christian IV. Beware that the city of Oslo, therefore, will be named «Kristiania» for most of this book.

Norway was neutral during World War I, but occupied by Germany 1940—1945. But now, I am moving way ahead. The story of *this* book's main character takes off decades before *both* World Wars – when Norway was still, on paper, under Swedish rule.

11 Østfold
12 Akershus
13 Oslo
14 Hedmark
15 Oppland
16 Buskerud
17 Vestfold
18 Telemark
19 Aust-Agder
20 Vest-Agder
21 Rogaland
22 Hordaland
23 Bergen
24 Sogn og Fjordane
25 Møre og Romsdal
26 Sør-Trøndelag
27 Nord-Trøndelag
28 Nordland
29 Troms
30 Finnmark

Map over Norway, with a list of the country's municipalities (prior to the municipality reform of 2020). For the purpose of this book, it's perhaps worth pointing out the locations of the following cities and towns: capital city Oslo (Kristiania 1624—1924), located in the municipality by the same name (13); Bergen, second largest city (23); third largest city, Trondheim, located in Sør-Trøndelag (26); the town of Drøbak, from where August Schønemann's parents emigrated in their youth, located in Akershus (12); the town Fredrikstad, where Schønemann appeared numerous times, located in Østfold (11). (Map from 1962.) (Nasjonalbiblioteket / The Norwegian National Library.)

Chapter 1

Paperer Pettersen

On February 18, 1925, the evening edition of the Norwegian daily *Aftenposten* (henceforth named «Norw. *Evening Post*») announced on its front page:

August Schønemann dead

Yes – it is really so. We shall never again witness his rubberlike countenance onstage, nor listen to his joyful jargon . . . August Schønemann possessed the rare gift, that he could bring a smile even to the lips of the grumpiest spectators; he served as the best medicine against the grayness of everyday life. . . He will be deeply missed by each and every one of us. . . . for he was a fine and decent man[,] and much beloved by a huge public, since he [as a comedian] had conquered a spot which, at the moment, no one else can fill.[2]

Carrying the tone of an obituary, the article was supplemented with a portrait of the esteemed star, taken at the time of his artistic peak; well-dressed, and with hat in hand, he gives us a slightly ambiguous smile, modest yet self-assured at the same time.

«The funeral is to be held at the Crematorium Tuesday, 24th [of February] at 2 ½,»[3] it was stated in an actual obituary notice a couple of days later, which was duly noted by readers. A massive crowd, consisting of colleagues and admirers alike, followed the comedy king to his grave that afternoon. One spectator reportedly remarked that August Schønemann had «generated crowds» up to the very last moment.[4]

With Schønemann's passing, the theaters and revue stages of Oslo – the city which had given up its old name of *Kristiania* just weeks prior – lost its greatest name and draw since the end of World War I. In his memory remained a few gramophone records and one 4-reel silent film, *Kjærlighet paa Pinde* (literal translation «Love on a Stick,» meaning «Lollipop») from 1922.

The 33-year old also left behind a baby daughter, two and a half-year old Aud.

***

The Trinity Church (Trefoldighetskirken) of Kristiania (now Oslo), probably late 1800s. Here, August Schønemann's parents, August Pettersen and Thrine Josefine Engebretsen, married in 1874. St. Olav's

Cathedral Church is seen farther up the street. (Nasjonalbiblioteket /
The Norwegian National Library.)

The locally famous Trinity Church at Hammersborg in Christiania (later Oslo) had been standing for 15 years when marriage was held between August Pettersen and Thrine Josefine Engebretsen in the spring of 1874.[5] Both were in their twenties – August b. 1845, Thrine Josefine b. 1851 – and had emigrated from the town of Drøbak to Norway's capital city several years prior.

Curiously, August Pettersen's father, b. 1814, carried the name of *August Frederik Schjønneman* (the spelling varies somewhat in legal documents),[6] an «office clerk»[7] who in 1840 had married 22-year old *Berthe Marie Pettersen*[8] (sometimes spelled *Pedersen*). August Frederik Schjønnemann, on his part, was the «illegitimate» son of sub-officer *Jonathan Frederik Schjønneman* (b. 1791, for years employed at Akershus Fortress, Norway) and «maid» *Berthe Marie Adolphsdatter*[9] (the couple married shortly after the arrival of their first son, had a total of at least ten children, and for years resided at Øvre Slottsgt. – «Upper Castle Street» – of central Christiania).

«Sub-officer» Jonathan Frederik was the son of a wigmaker, *Kield Schønnemand* (d. 1798) and *Anna Joachima Mørch* (d. 1800).

Probably originating from Prussia, and literally meaning «beautiful», variations on the name «Schonemann» can be traced in Norwegian records at least as far back as the 1500s.[10]

Whatever caused August Pettersen to use, for his surname, his *mother's maiden name*, is not clear – such was not the norm at the time – but limited contact between father and son is a possible explanation. He *is* listed as «August Schønemand» in the 1865 census for Kristiania,[11] but was, as far as the author can tell, to use «Pettersen» permanently after his father's passing in 1872.[12] Carrying the surname of «Pettersen», he would not particularly stand out with his name. As anyone may well guess, in Norway, Pettersen is about as common a name as «Peterson» in the United States, whereas «Schønemann» remains quite rare to this day. (To make matters not exactly less confusing, he is listed as August *Petersen*, single *t*, in the marriage certificate of 1874,[13] but this seems to be an error. Prior to the 20th century, the spelling of names was not treated as an exact science, as we shall also see later.)

August Pettersen's wife, the aforementioned Thrine Josefine Engebretsen, was the daughter of Johannes Engebretsen and Ane Engebretsen (b. Gulbransen),[14] and grew up with two sisters (as of the 1865 census) in comfortable middleclass conditions.

Although young at the time, August Pettersen was not an untried card on the job market upon his marriage, having been hired by the wallpaper company Ramberg & Co upon its establishment in 1870. During its first few years, Ramberg & Co primarily provided stable gear to customers, a service which could be trusted to generate a decent livelihood, at a time when horse and wagon was a common way of transportation. (He found himself referred to as «saddler» in marriage notices in the papers.[15]) The firm was located in central Christiania (Øvre Slottsgt. 16), and could soon offer services of all kinds related to transportation and decoration. Both «travel effects», collars, and padded drawing-room furniture were part of their assortment, «All of the latest fashion», of course.[16]

When the firm's founder, Rasmus Ramberg, passed away in 1898, it went without saying that the same August Pettersen would keep the business running, and along with colleague Julius Ungersnæss, he had the firm renamed to «Pettersen & Ungersnæss».[17] However, he eventually left the firm to begin anew solely under his own name, and, for the remainder of his life, August Pettersen kept a similar store by himself in Akersgt. of central Christiania,[18] right nearby what, with time, would develop into the governmental quarters of Norway.

August Pettersen became a well-known and respected person of his trade. There exist reports claiming that he had a central role in the decoration preparations before the crowning of both Swedish-Norwegian king Oscar II, and Norwegian king Haakon VII (in 1872 and 1905, respectively).[19]

It seems clear, from the various apartments in which the older August Pettersen resided up to his passing, that he as a man of rural background grew relatively comfortable with city life, and we may assume the same to have been true for his wife, Thrine Josefine. The couple initially settled down in the neighborhood of Grünerløkka, in an apartment at Markveien 52.[20] Although by the 2010s, Grünerløkka had turned into one of the more expensive areas to live in Oslo – becoming known as a «hip» neighborhood, one might say, rife with coffeeshops and a vivid city life – in the late 1800s it was considered working-class territory, and mostly associated with factories. Of course, a few lower middleclass households such as the Pettersen family also resided there, for practical or other reasons. With time, the family moved to a second-floor apartment in Sofienberggt. 2A,[21] also at Grünerløkka.

August Pettersen Jr., later known as Schønemann, and his sister Berthe Marie. C. 1900. (Nasjonalbiblioteket / The Norwegian National Library.)

A year after the couple's union, in 1875, Thrine Josefine gave birth to her first child, a boy given the name of Birger Olaf Johannes.[22] The infant mortality rate being very high at the time, the child sadly died about a year later.[23] Six more children were to arrive within the next sixteen years, three boys and three girls: *Anna* Augusta Maranda (1877);[24] *Agnes* Mathea Johanna (1879);[25] *Frithjof* Jens (1883; curiously listed as «Jens Frithof *Schjønnemann*» in the birth certificate,[26] as the only one of the children *not* named «Pettersen» upon birth, for whatever reason); *Olaf* (1885); *Berthe* Marie (1887),[27] likely named after her paternal grandmother; and finally, on May 30, 1891, August Pettersen Jr. saw the light of day. Why the parents decided to «wait» until the fourth-born son before reusing the father's forename in the family, is not clear, but perhaps the strong-willed father hoped that the name of August could serve as a sort of guardian angel to the boy. Being undernourished at birth, the family feared for August Jr.'s life at first, especially given that his three older brothers had suffered from poor health since early on. As noted above, their first-born son Birger Olaf Johannes only reached his first year, and the younger Olaf also died before August Jr.'s birth, at the age of five in late 1890.[28] Frithjof Jens was to pass away in March 1900 at the age of 16.[29]

The three girls, Anna, Agnes and Berthe, were all to reach adulthood, fortunately. Anna married at twenty in 1897, to «trade agent»[30] Georg Emil Petersen.[31] Agnes wed bank clerk Fredrik Pedersen a few years later,[32] meaning that Berthe Marie and August Jr. were the only remaining siblings in the Pettersen household for much of their childhood.

Despite the family's understandable worries concerning his health, August Jr. thankfully survived the crucial childhood years, and is said to have grown into a charming and imaginative child. By one account, he was treated as the «leader» among friends in his childhood quarters, always quick to come up with ideas for pranks (some of which almost sound as if borrowed from a silent film comedy, with a furious cop chasing the unruly urchins).[33]

Excerpt from school photo, late 1890s. August Jr. seated to the right. (Nasjonalbiblioteket / The Norwegian National Library.)

August Jr. had a short walk to school, unlike many other children of the time, but schoolwork didn't interest him much. From early on, dreams of *performing* took up most of his hours.

Notes

2.   *Aftenposten*, evening edition, February 18, 1925, p. 1.

3.   *Aftenposten*, morning edition, February 20, 1925, p. 7.

4.   Kvist, Per: *Når katten er ute... – Chat Noir 1912-1942* (Det Mallingske Boktrykkeri, 1942), p. 32.

5.   *Christiania Intelligentssedler*, June 11, 1874, p. 2. See also *Dagbladet*, June 12, 1874, p. 3.

6.   Church book from Garnisonsmenigheten parish, Akershus slottsmenighet local parish 1810-1814. (SAO, Garnisonsmenigheten Kirkebøker, SAO/A-10846/G/Ga/L0002 Parish register (copy) no. 2, 1810-1814, p. 154-155.)

7.   Burials: 1872-12-30. Church book from Krohgstøtten sykehus (hospital) parish 1865-1873 (0301E5). (SAO, Krohgstøtten sykehus Kirkebøker, SAO/A-10854/F/Fa/L0001 Parish register (official), no. 1, 1865-1873, p. 150.)

8.   Married: 1840-09-29. Church book from Oslo Hospital's congregation 1829-1849. (SAO, Gamlebyen prestekontor Kirkebøker, SAO/A-10884/F/Fa/L0003Parish register (official) no. 3, 1829-1849, p. 274.) Note: the frequent reuse of names in families back then sometimes makes it a cumbersome task to investigate family records. In the marriage register, the groom "Fredrik Schønneman" is said to have "Fredrik Schjønemann" for a father. When coupled with other finds in church books, I have concluded this, and several other factors, must make this the "correct" Berthe Marie Pettersen/Pedersen.

9.   Churck book from Garnisonsmenigheten parish. G7Ga/L0002: Klokkerbok No. 2, 1810-1814, p. 154.

10. See *Bergen Borgerbog. 1: 1550-1751* (Werner & Co.s Bogtrykkeri, 1878).

11. 1865 census for Kristiania. 0159 Skippergaden.

12. Burials: 1872-12-30. Church book from Krohgstøtten sykehus (hospital) parish 1865-1873 (0301E5).

13. Marriages: 1874-05-06. SAO, Trefoldighet prestekontor Kirkebøker, SAO/A-10882/F/Fc/L0002 Parish register (official) no III 2, 1874-1881, p. 2.

14. Census 1865 for 0203B Drøbak prestegjeld, Drøbak kjøpstad. Arkivref. RA/S-2231.

15. *Christiania Intelligentssedler*, June 11, 1874, p. 2.

16. *Aftenposten*, June 16, 1883, p. 4.

17. *Norsk Kundegjørelsestidende*, February 1, 1898, p. 1.

18. *Aftenposten*, morning edition, November 24, 1907, p. 3.

19. *Aftenposten*, morning edition, December 17, 1913, p. 6.

20. Census 1875 for 0301 Kristiania kjøpstad. Arkivref. RA/S-2231/E.

21. Census 1900 for 0301 Kristiania kjøpstad. Arkivref. RA/S-2231/E.

22. Births and baptisms: 1875-05-06. Church book from Paulus parish 1875-1878 (0301M16). (SAO, Paulus prestekontor Kirkebøker, SAO/A-10871/F/Fa/L0001Parish register (official) no. 1, 1875-1878, p. 10.) Note: according to some accounts online, the first-born son was named Berger, which I also use in the Norwegian version of this book; however, the birth notice in church books lists him as 'Birger', as does the obituary notice cited below.

23. *Aftenposten*, July 1, 1876, p. 2. Obituary notice.

24. Births and baptisms: 1877-08-12. Church book from Paulus parish 1875-1878 (0301M16). (SAO, Paulus prestekontor Kirkebøker, SAO/A-10871/G/Ga/L0001Klokkerbok nr. 1, 1875-1878, p. 85.)

25. Census 1891 for 0301 Kristiania. Note: Agnes' name was sometimes given as 'Agnis' in legal papers; they weren't always so pedantic about the spelling of names back in the day.

26. Births and baptisms: 1883-08-13. Church book from Trefoldighet parish 1881-1891 (0301M22). (SAO, Trefoldighet prestekontor Kirkebøker, SAO/A-10882/F/Fa/L0005Parish register (official) no. I 5, 1881-1891, p. 120.)

27. Census 1891 for 0301 Kristiania.

28. *Aftenposten*, morning edition, November 5, 1890, p. 2. Obituary notice.

29. *Social-Demokraten*, March 3, 1900, p. 3. Frithjof is here said to have been "15 years, 6 months" upon his death, but he had in fact reached his 16th birthday at the time. Frithjof is named «Frithjof Jens Schjønnemann Pettersen» in the obituary notice.

30. Described as such («*handelsfullmektig*») in marriage notice, *Morgenbladet*, August 12, 1897, p. 3.

31. Church book from Paulus parish 1891-1901 (0301M16). (SAO, Paulus prestekontor Kirkebøker, SAO/A-10871/F/Fa/L0009Parish register (official) no. 9, 1891-1901, p. 112.)

32. Birth certificate to Agnes' and Fredrik Pedersen's son Rolf, 1905-12-10. Church book from Trefoldighet parisah 1899-1914 (0301M22). (SAO, Trefoldighet prestekontor Kirkebøker, SAO/A-10882/F/Fa/L0007Parish register (official) no. I 7, 1900-1914, p. 144.)

33. Hagen, Kai (editor): *Byen vår – Glimt av Oslo gjennom 900 år* (Herman Ruuds forlag, 1948), p. 168.

Chapter 2

Tormentors & Twist

«*The souls to be expelled from the company of the bourgeois, were the students, cadets, salesmen – and actors. These four castes were banned from the 'good company', among such people one could not socialize.*»34
 – Johannes Brun, Norwegian actor (1832-1890).

The late 1800s are typically referred to as a turbulent time in much of Europe, known as an era marked by great changes and upheavals, and the same is true of Norway, to some degree. The introduction of parliamentarism in Norway in 1884, followed by the end of the Norwegian-Swedish union in 1905, are just two of several well-known events which affected the increasingly industrialized and urbanized country of Norway during this period. Politician Johannes Steen of the Norwegian Liberal Party (*Venstre*) had just been elected prime minister in the year of August Jr's birth (1891); the Liberal Party was to remain one of the two large political parties to serve in Norway during August Jr's lifetime, the other being the Conservative Party (*Høyre*).

Obligatory schooling in Norway – literally called *folk school* at this time – was confined to children between 7 and 14 years of age.

Electricity was slowly being introduced in the capital city, but gas and paraffin was still used for lighting more often. August Jr was four years of age when the first petrol-powered automobile in the country, a Bentz, was put into operation, carrying passengers over short distances. Motion-pictures were in its earliest, most intricate phase; the first Kinematograph (movie theater) in the country was opened in 1904, but the first true «movie stars» did not emerge until several years later. Instead, theaters and, in rural areas, traveling acting ensembles remained the most popular means of entertainment to most people.

Whereas one typically associates light stage entertainment of the late 19th and early 20th century in America with «vaudeville» – and «music hall» in Great Britain – in Norway and the rest of Scandinavia there was, in particular, much talk about «revues» around this time. («Revues» were also very much a thing elsewhere as well, of course, the States and Great Britain included; Scandinavia was not unique in that regard.) As with vaudeville and music hall, it is practically impossible to determine at what point the modern revue was «invented». It has been argued that some of Aristophanes' plays, with their use of choral singing, may qualify as a kind of revue,[35] but surely this wide definition of the term demands a great amount of good-will. It would be somewhat akin to proposing that the illustrated, European humor magazines of the 1800s can be regarded as early examples of *comic strips* – there may be similarities to be found, in terms of format, but the end result is still so different from the first modern comic strips which appeared in the States (*The Katzenjammer Kids,* etc.), that the comparison, in the end, becomes misleading. «Revue» as a fully realized, intentional entertainment model did not truly develop until the mid-19th century, and several more decades passed before it was widely established across country borders.

As such, the first hints of modern revue in Norway can be traced relatively far back in history, which is surprising, considering that the operation of professional theater, for a long while, was limited here, partly because of our shared history with Denmark up to 1814. While Danish theater enjoyed a brief «golden age» in the early 1700s, largely due to the influence of famous playwright Ludvig Holberg (d. 1754), this was brought to an abrupt end as the deeply religious king Christian VI of Denmark-Norway came to power, and practically banned professional theater operation in the country. Fortunately, his son and heir to the throne, Frederic V, felt very differently about theater than his father, and allowed the «playhouses» to reopen once he came to power, towards the end of playwright Holberg's life.

Even so, Danish theater life proved unable to be duplicated in Norway. Arenas for performing eventually flourished in Norway as well, of course, but a *systematic* operation of theaters was far more scarce. However, in 1827, the Christiania Public Theater opened its doors, while the more broadly popular Klingenberg Great Salon (also located in the capital city) experienced a dawning golden age. The latter stage would offer an incalculable amount of comic performances in the following years, arranged in a way which must be said to carry similarities to modern revues, however broadly. Revue expert Haakon B. Nielson singles out the sketch *New Year's Eve 1848-1849* as one example of a very early, «revue-like» performance in Norway.[36] Announcements of similar performances can be found with frequency in Norwegian press in the decade that followed.[37] At this early point, Norwegian comedy writers primarily took inspiration from the «New Year performances» of Paris; for a while, comedy playwrights of France had developed a tradition of doing shameless satire over the most notable events and scandals of the bygone year. Again by Nielson's account, the first true, «fully-Norwegian» revue production saw the light of day in 1872.

Even so, the first true revue «stars» of Norway did not come about until around the turn of the 20th century. Certain prominent revue playwrights and popular performers emerged with time, of course, but one can hardly say that comic superstars comparable to Herbert Campbell (d. 1904), Charles Coborn (1852-1945), or Harry

«Little Tich» Relph (1867-1928) of Great Britain were to be found here – until the early 1900s, that is. Norwegian comedian Adolf Østbye (1868-1907) may be an early candidate, but he did not reach the peak of his fame until around 1900. (Today, Østbye is chiefly remembered as the first Norwegian «record artist»; there exist phonograph cylinders by him from as early as 1889.)

Outdoors performance of a comedy play or sketch at Homansbyen, Christiania (now Oslo), late 1890s/early 1900s. Actor with silk hat to the right is comedian and character actor Bernt Johannessen (1859-1907), the other players unidentified. (Photo: Severin Worm-Petersen / Norwegian Museum of Science and Technology. This work is licensed under the Creative Commons Attribution-ShareAlike 4.0 International License. To view a copy of this license, visit http://creativecommons. org/licenses/by-sa/4.0/ or send a letter to Creative Commons, PO Box 1866, Mountain View, CA 94042, USA.)

For decades, the unwritten «headquarters» of Norwegian theater life remained in the area surrounding the Christiania Public Theater, a part of the city known as 'The Bank Square.' Understandably so, given that many of the city's prominent citizens lived in the neighborhood at that time.[38]

Small part of Christiania Tivoli seen to the left; entrance of The Norwegian National Theater (Nasjonalteatret) to the right. Early 1900s. (Nasjonalbiblioteket / The Norwegian National Library.)

This began to change by the late 19th century, however. In 1877, Christiania Tivoli – perhaps best translated to *The Christiania Amusement Quarter* – was completed, located in an area of the city known as Viken/Vika (today, Oslo City Hall stands there). Furthermore, with the opening of the National Theater in 1899, theater life moved towards the center of the city,[39] around an area known as *Karl Johan* (named after a Swedish king who'd fought in the Napoleonic wars). Other theaters were established in this area with time, such as Chat Noir and Eldorado.

"Karl Johans gate," main street of Kristiania (now Oslo), with the Royal Castle in the distance, 1920s. A brief walk from there, Kristiania theater life blossomed in the late 1800s and early 1900s. Photo: Birgit 'Bibby' Mathiesen (1908-1990). (Author's collection.)

Eventually, by the late 1910s and 1920s, the *revue format* had transformed into a «respectable» kind of entertainment, known for being often sophisticated, colorful, and gorgeous-looking, something which even upper middleclass citizens could enjoy without embarrassment. However, such was not the case initially. The many prejudices against comedians, comic singers, and other «flippant» entertainers remained difficult to overcome for performers.

***

How did it come to be that August Jr. grew so infatuated with the glow of footlights? It remains unclear exactly when he was bit by the *acting bug*, and, despite showing signs of great imagination and playfulness at a young age, it was far from evident that he would wind up a professional performer. Like the undisputed «king» of Swedish revue of the same era, *Ernst Rolf* (also b. 1891), August Jr.

did not come from an «actors'» home, but, similar to Ernst Rolf, he proved to possess talent in that regard from early on. Revue expert Haakon B. Nielson claims August to have made his professional stage debut at 15, «an evening in the fall of 1906», at Østre Teater (Eastern Theater) of Grønlandsleiret, Kristiania, doing the one-act play *Portnerens plageaander* («The Janitor's Tormentors»),[40] but the Kristiania press does not seem to have taken notice.

On the other hand, August himself claimed, in later interviews, to have made his acting debut at 16, in a stage adaptation of *Oliver Twist*, directed by well-known theater director Jakob von der Lippe. However, August's own scrapbook does not include any notice of his alleged appearances in *Oliver Twist*, as far as the author can tell. It is indeed correct that director von der Lippe went on tour with *Oliver Twist* in the fall of 1907 and throughout the following spring,[41] but my attempts to find proof of August's involvement in the production have been futile. This is not to say that it could not very well be true; in fact, yours truly believes there is reason to take August's word for it, as he recalled on at least *two* separate occasions to have played in *Oliver Twist* (in interviews done in 1913 and 1922, respectively).[42] Granted, actors of his generation were infamous for embellishing the truth to eager reporters, but it seems perhaps unlikely that August would've seen any reason to «invent» such a specific detail (of relatively minor importance) on several occasions. Perhaps he did a small, uncredited part in the play. We can, however, say with certainty that he did *not* play the title role in *Oliver Twist* that early on in his career.

Whether or not he appeared in *Oliver Twist* in 1907, August was undoubtedly a performer of some experience by that point. In addition to his role in the brief play *The Janitor's Tormentors*, the bold teenager performed comic songs at Vestre Teater (Western Theater) in the busy street of Bogstadvn. 12, housed in a classy building which, with time, would come to screen motion-pictures.

Bogstadveien, one of Kristiania's busy quarters. A bit farther up the street (Bogstadvn. 12), Schønemann performed comic songs as a teenager, at Vestre Teater (Western Theater). This snapshot from the 1920s. Photo: Birgit 'Bibby' Mathiesen (1908-1990). (Author's collection.)

It's only reasonable to assume, though, that young August did not yet truly *captivate* audiences, as he was to do in later years. Like most performers, he cut his teeth doing pretty much whatever roles came his way. However, very rarely does he seem to have truly «flopped» onstage, even this early on in his career.

Like many aspiring actors, the young man found himself obliged to find a sidejob to make ends meet, and he worked for a while as a clerk in a draper store, perhaps after being recommended by his father. 1907 offered small, but important steps of progress in terms of acting jobs; among other things, he appeared in a couple of plays at the Norwegian Students Society of Kristiania, such as the beloved «singing play» *Til sæters* («*To the Mountain Pastures*»), penned by Claus Pavels Riis. (Many years later, in 1924, August was asked to appear in director Harry Ivarsons' film adaptation of this play, but health issues sadly came in the way. More on this later.)

Theater reviewers were not much interested in student theater, however, so none of the aforementioned plays received any press coverage.

Following this modest, but promising starting phase, August's acting career came to a temporary halt. Perhaps he kept on performing comic songs in Bogstadvn. 12 in the evenings, but by and large, he seems not to have been involved in any more theatrical activities for well over a year. One may assume this not to have been the result of a declining interest in the stage as such, but rather, he probably found it necessary to earn some dough fulltime. The «intermission» would soon be over, after which the young actor's career took off for real.

Notes

34. Heltberg, A.H.: *Muntre minner fra Norsk Teaterliv* (Norden forlag, 1944), p. 7.

35. Kvist, Per: *Når katten er ute...*, p. 21.

36. Nielson, Haakon B.: *Revystjerner i 1920-årenes Kristiania* (J.W. Cappelens forlag, 1970), p. 12.

37. *Christiania Intelligentssedler*, February 6, 1852, p. 1.

38. Although several buildings from as far back as the 1600s still stand around the 'Bank Square', today the area largely houses various offices, galleries, and the like.

39. Bang-Hansen, Odd: *Chat Noir og Norsk Revy* (J.W. Cappelens forlag, 1961), pp. 24-25.

40. Nielson, p. 17.

41. See, for instance, *Tvedestrandsposten* August 24, 1907, and *Fredrikstad Tilskuer* January 8, 1908.

42. *Kongsberg Dagblad*, July 1, 1913, and *Aftenposten*, morning edition, June 12, 1922. The director in question is Jakob von der Lippe (1870-1954), for many years costume designer at Norway's National Theater, although the name is spelled as *Jacob* in the article.

Chapter 3

Charley's Aunt

Nearly two years went by before teenager August Jr again seized the stage – there is, at least, no evidence to suggest otherwise – when he again got a taste of the footlights, in the late fall of 1908. On November 27, he appeared in two 1-act plays in the small town of Kristiansund (quite a distance away from the capital city), staged at the «Music Association's Bazaar».[43] Not only had he made his comeback onstage; the roles assigned him were not insignificant.

Granted, the first of the two plays was perhaps not that much to speak about, a by now forgotten «singing play» entitled *Onkels kjærlighed* («Uncle's Love»). The second play was all the more noteworthy, however, as August received a role in Brandon Thomas' famous farce, *Charley's Aunt* (*possibly* the title role, but yours truly cannot say for sure). By now a classic comedy since long ago, the farce had appeared on the stages of Europe and America alike for only about a decade and a half in 1908, at a time when it still held the reputation of being somewhat *risqué*. The main character, a cheerful male student, is convinced to pose as the aunt of a classmate, to serve as chaperone for a couple of friends while they're on a date. Complications arise when an older man visiting their school finds himself attracted to the «aunt» (or, perhaps, to her alleged wealth).

Later immortalized through a number of film adaptations, starring such talents as Sydney Chaplin (1925), Jack Benny (1941), and others, it's regrettable that August's involvement in *Charley's Aunt* could not be captured on film. «*Charley's aunt* did tremendous success yesterday evening,» one local paper declared, adding that the play would be performed once more due to public demand.[44]

Still, the most notable fact related to August's performances in Kristiansund, actually had to do with his name in the theater credits. The 17-year old had here abandoned his legal surname «Pettersen», and was instead billed as «Aug. Schønneman», a variation on his paternal grandfather's surname. That the young actor chose to do so, is perhaps not so surprising. He probably reckoned that a pseudonym could serve as an advantage to him in the field of acting, perhaps in the belief that there existed «a sort of magic in a *nom de guerre*,» as Norwegian novelist Johan Borgen once put it in a novel.[45] As seen in Chapter 1, one of August Jr.'s brothers was baptized «Jens Frithof Schjønnemann» in 1883 (and was listed as «Schjønnemann Pettersen» in a newspaper death notice, upon his tragic passing in 1900), so the name had evidently not been *entirely* abandoned in the family through the years. We may wonder what August Pettersen *Senior* thought of August Jr's «new» choice of name, though. Whether the father made a fuss, or was perfectly fine with it, is anybody's guess.

But completely certain of his new stage name, young August was not. When he, in March 1909, signed a contract with the Norwegian Theater Company (*Det norske Teaterselskab*), the actor chose to, again, go under his legal surname in the theater credits.

The roots of the Norwegian Theater Company could be traced back to the 19th century. By 1909, the company had become known for staging «good dramatic literature with talented performers, touring various Norwegian communities.»[46] Signing his contract with the company, August was obliged to appear at a theater in the suburb of Drammen (about a half hour's train ride away from the capital city today) each Sunday for the next eight weeks, starting March 7, 1909 and concluding towards the end of April, «for a Salary of 5 Crowns» per week (approximately $41.30 in today's currency; not a princely sum, but in the eyes of young August, it was an offer he couldn't refuse). The company paid for his travel expenses, to and from Kristiania—Drammen.[47]

August's employment at the Norwegian Theater Company proved to be a turning point in his career. For the first time, he was contractually tied to a theater. The engagement turned out to be brief, however. On March 14, he appeared in the Swedish 6-act play, *Wermlændingerne*, in the role of a servant. A week thereafter, another «folk comedy» came his way, *Andersen, Pettersen, Lundstrøm*, in which August played a tailor's apprentice.

By the end of the engagement, his opportunities broadened somewhat, as playwright Ludvig Holberg's immortal comedy-drama, *Jeppe on the Hill* from 1722, was performed in a couple of suburban towns (Tønsberg and Drammen), on April 18 and May 4, respectively.[48] Considered a poignant political satire of its time, and one of the most cherished plays of the Danish-Norwegian literary canon, in *Jeppe* Holberg depicted the misfortunes of an alcoholic peasant by the same name, with one famous line declaring: «They always talk about Jeppe *drinking* . . . but they never ask *why* Jeppe drinks!» August did two separate roles in the staging of the play, among them that of a tax collector's wife.[49]

Relative success notwithstanding, a contract renewal with the Norwegian Theater Company did not come August's way. To the public at large, he was still an unknown, being not yet 18 years of age.

While spring of 1909 blossomed, August again found himself without any steady acting work. Random freelance jobs came his way, from time to time, but the pay was slight. He later recalled to have been paid, at best, «500 Øre» (500 Cent) doing such odd jobs, and only in the weekends.[50] For the remainder of the week, he had to find another «ordinary» trade of work for himself; this time around, he wound up serving as a warehouse assistant, at a men's clothing shop. August still lived at home, although by now, the family had moved yet again, to a first-floor apartment in St. Olavsgt 5,[51] a couple of stone's throws away from the Trinity Church at which his parents had once been declared husband and wife. Although not considered one of the very «best» parts of the city, their move from Grünerløkka clearly indicates that the family now enjoyed a rather decent livelihood – and August Sr. only had a brief walk to work.

By 1910, Schønemann's family had moved to this house at St. Olavs gt. 5 in central Kristiania (now Oslo), residing in a first-floor apartment. (In the building to the left, famous Norwegian architect Wilhelm von Hanno (1826—82) lived for several years.) (Photo by the author, 2020s.)

Although August's oldest sisters, Anna and Agnes, had moved away from home since long ago, his youngest sister, Berthe, still remained with August and their parents. Notably, Berthe is described as «actress» in the census of the time.[52] Stage ambitions were, in other words, not confined to the mind of August Jr the in the family; perhaps his sister had had some influence on him in that regard, being four years older. Like her brother, Berthe was also to adopt the surname of Schønemann as an adult, as we shalll see later.

From his time as a warehouse assistant, August recalled with glee that he never put his stage ambitions away, not even while being stuck in the dull warehouse in the store basement. «Of course I, like any actor, also wished to do tragedy,» August reminisced, «and I can remember so well . . . when I walked down the basement to practice various roles, with all kinds of inventory serving as my 'audience.'»[53]

August's confession to have wished, as a youngster, to play tragic material, not just comedy, puts him in the company of several other, great «funny-men», Charlie Chaplin among them.[54] As it turned out, the truly big, dramatic roles would remain absent throughout August's career – alas, as far as we know, he never played Strindberg, Chekhov or Ibsen – but, towards the end of his life, adoring audiences were to witness him dressed up as «Hamlet» at last.

Notes

43. Theater program + Aug. Schønemann's personal commentary, stored in his scrapbook, ca. 1909. «Musikkforeningens Basar.»

44. *Romsdals Amtstidende*, November 30, 1908, p. 3.

45. Borgen, Johan (1956): *De mørke kilder* (Den norske Bokklubben, 1989 edition, p. 88). Notably, in the same novel, which is set in the 1910s and 20s as the second volume of Borgen's *Lillelord* trilogy, August Schønemann is briefly given a mention, described as "the scrawny deity of Kristiania humor . . ." Translated by yours truly.

46. Bødtkers, Sigurd: *Kristiania-premiérer gjennem 30 aar* (H. Aschehoug & Co., 1929), p. 65.

47. Handwritten contract stored in Aug. Schønemann's scrapbook, ca. 1909. See also Nielson, p. 18.

48. Theater program stored in Aug. Schønemann's scrapbook, 1909.

49. Theater program + Schønemann's handwritten commentary in his scrapbook, 1909.

50. Nielson, p. 19.

51. Census 1910 for 0301 Kristiania kjøpstad. Arkivref. RA/S-2231/E/Ef.

52. Ibid.

53. *Kongsberg Dagblad*, July 1, 1913.

54. Hayes, Kevin J. (editor): *Charlie Chaplin Interviews* (University Press of Mississippi, 2005), p. 4. Interview with Chaplin from 1915.

Chapter 4

Fahlstrøm and Qværnstrøm

Fortunately, August's unexciting period at the warehouse soon came to an end. In August 1909, a few months after his contract with «Det norske Teaterselskab» expired, he could again boast of another steady theater job to his family over dinner. Granted, this time he was not primarily expected to display his talents onstage; instead, he'd become the new prompter of Fahlstrøm's Theater.[55]

Married couple Johan and Alma Fahlstrøm's variety theater had been running for six years upon August's employment, being located at Torvgt. 9 (central Kristiania). The couple was widely known in theater circles. Johan (b. 1867) had made his debut onstage at 20, and appeared several times at the Norwegian National Theater, before he and his wife decided to open their own venue (or, arguably, they saw it *necessary* to do so, as the temperamental Johan is said to not have been on always good terms with a number of other notable theater personalities of the time). Reportedly, their theater could room a total of 2,000 people. Johan was also a talented painter and sculptor; a selection of his work has been exhibited at the Norwegian National Gallery. Alma (b. 1863), who was raised in both Norway and Sweden, became known as a talented actress and instructor. (She was also sister to actress Harriet Bosse, third and final wife to world-renowned Swedish playwright and author August Strindberg.)

Alma and Johan Fahlstrøm appearing in a stage adaptation of Henrik Ibsen's 'Terje Vigen,' probably 1905. (Photo: Anders Beer Wilse / Oslo Museum.)

As it turned out, the days of Fahlstrøm theater were numbered, as the couple found its operation both increasingly exhausting and costly, but its shutdown still belonged to the future when young August first entered their theater lobby as an untried prompter, in the late summer of 1909.

To serve as prompter may not have been a dream job to August, but he quickly proved to be very adept at the task. It made for good practice, and, perhaps even more crucial: he became part of a theatrical environment «for real», made friends and acquaintances for whom he happily performed, whenever an opportunity arose. An actor at the theater fondly recalled August's impersonation of «*Lehmann on Skates*» during lunch breaks.[56] Few readers may get this reference, understandably: «Lehmann» was the Norwegian nickname given French comedian André Deed, who, in a seemingly endless stream of brief silent films churned out by the studio of Pathé, had reached world fame a few years prior. However, yours truly is tempted to ask if it may not be more likely that August actually impersonated *another* French film comedian during these breaks; the even more famous Max Linder (1883-1925). Linder, of course, was also connected to Pathé's studio, and indeed, one of his many films carried the name of *Max veut apprendre à patiner* (1907) – or, in English, *Max Wants to Skate*. That August must've been aware of Linder and his films, we can at least safely assume.

Comic plays were one of Fahlstrøm's specialties. During August's stint as prompter there, the theater staged numerous comedies, among them a play by famous Swedish playwright Gustaf af Geijerstam,[57] *Pikernes Alfred* («*Alfred the Ladies Man*»),[58] as well as the operetta *The Dollar Princess* with music by Austrian composer Leo Fall.[59] Serving as the leading star in most of their productions, Fahlstrøm theater was blessed with talented actor Hauk Aabel. Although later primarily known as the father to one of Norway's most iconic actors, Per Aabel (1901-1999), father Hauk was a major draw to audiences in his own right in the early 1900s.

Fahlstrøm also staged the tragedy *Quo Vadis?* around this time, based on Henryk Sienkieqicz's famous novel set in Emperor Nero's era, in which August even received a minor role onstage, as an executed Christian man – but the young actor proved unwilling to depart from the world of (admittedly slightly morbid) comedy for that reason. His close friend, Per Kvist, recalled that, as August portrayed the tragically executed soul being carried out on a stretcher onstage, he suddenly arose from the stretcher and gave fellow actor Johan Fahlstrøm a sly look, whereupon the «murdered» young man somberly uttered: «When the dead awakens. . .» – and dropped dead on the stretcher. Fahlstrøm, being behind the scenes at that moment, reportedly had to let the public wait for his return onstage longer than intended, as he just couldn't stop laughing.[60]

Towards the end of Fahlstrøm theater's time, their acting troupe embarked on a tour of Trondheim (third largest city of Norway, after Kristiania and Bergen) in May 1911, to perform a total of three operettas. (Although historian Haakon B. Nielson writes that the tour took place shortly *after* the theater's permanent shutdown,[61] Fahlstrøm Theater's official farewell performance was withheld until the tour of Trondheim had completed its run.)

The first production to be staged in Trondheim, had already been performed by Fahlstrøm's troupe in Kristiania the month prior, to great acclaim: Sir George Dance's well-known musical, *A Chinese Honeymoon* from 1899. For decades one of the most beloved musicals to be staged in much of Europe, the play's popularity was eventually to wane after World War II, in part due to its use of «ethnic stereotypes» which audiences of today may find problematic. However, when staged by Fahlstrøm's troupe in Trondheim, in the spring of 1911, the response was enthusiastic.[62]

To August personally, the tour was of special importance. By now, he served not only as Fahlstrøm's always reliable prompter – he also received notable roles onstage. In the case of *A Chinese*

Honeymoon, though, he wound up at the very bottom of the credits list (again billed as «August Pettersen»), but by the second production in Trondheim, things improved, as he received a large role as a private, in the 3-act operetta *Høstmanøver («Fall Maneuver»)*. Following a particularly satisfying performance of *Fall Maneuver*, August was apparently bestowed with a large bouquet of flowers for his interpretation of the role, to the «great envy» of «the leading lady and other actors.»[63] Even more notably: from *Fall Maneuver* onwards, he was to be billed as *August Schønemann* for good.

Schønemann in the operetta Høstmanøver (Fall Maneuver), spring 1911. (Nasjonalbiblioteket / The Norwegian National Library.)

Being in vogue at the time, yet another operetta was staged in Trondheim before the troupe's breakup: the 3-act *Zigeunerliebe*, penned by Austrian playwright Robert Bodanzky. Its world premiére having taken place just the year before, *Zigeunerliebe* included music written by the, in his time, celebrated composer Franz Lehár (of *Merry Widow* fame). Playing a «handsome peasant boy», August once again received praise for his acting, by his own account.[64]

Nonetheless, audiences' thirst for operettas – or Fahlstrøm's acting troupe – seem to have had a limit. Whereas the first production of the tour, *A Chinese Honeymoon*, had received exstensive coverage in the local press, newspapers accorded *Fall Maneuver* and *Zigeunerliebe* scarce mention. Critics may have assumed the news value of Fahlstrøm's visit in Trondheim to have waned, once *A Chinese Honeymoon* was done with.

On the other hand, Fahlstrøm theater's farewell performance in Kristiania, held in late August 1911, received widespread attention, in nationwide papers at that. On its front page the following day, the Norw. *Evening Post* proclaimed the theater's final show to have consisted of «an unusually joyful and evocative evening, [and] the crowded house expressed great affection towards the Fahlstrøm couple and the theater itself, through applause which took the form of ovations after each performance.»[65] Other than the Fahlstrøm couple, actor Hauk Aabel received particular notice. In what capacity August Schønemann participated throughout the theater's ceremonious farewell that evening, is unclear.

Following the closure of their theater, Johan and Alma Fahlstrøm's interest in theater operation seems to have faded, although they continued to occasionally perform in succeeding years. Tragically, less than a year after Fahlstrøm theater's «farewell performance», the couple's son, 18-year old Arne, died in the sinking of the «RMS *Titanic*». He'd been on his way to the USA to study film. After this, the couple reportedly bequeathed their entire fortune to the Norwegian Society for Sea Rescue.

By fall 1911, 20-year old August Schønemann found himself thrown back into the world of freelancing. Even so, he was in a position much different than before. With his successful phase at Fahlstrøm theater behind him, it didn't take long for another major opportunity to come his way. In early October, he signed another contract, this time with the *Kristiania Folk Theater*, managed by another established actor of the day, Pehr Qværnstrøm. Conveniently, Schønemann's new workplace resided just a few blocks away from his previous workplace, at Torvgt. 14.[66] (Kristiania Folk Theater is not to be confused with another theater by a similar name, still in operation but located elsewhere in the city.)

The Folk Theater's manager, Pehr Qværnstrøm, was a man of many talents. The very fall he found himself greeting newcomer August hello for the first time at his theater, Qværnstrøm appeared in two silent films. First, he starred in the drama *Fattigdommens forbandelse* (*The Curse of Poverty*), in retrospect often singled out as the first noteworthy fiction film to have been produced in Norway. Shortly thereafter, Qværnstrøm appeared onscreen yet again, in *Bondefangeri i Vaterland* (*Peasant Trapping in Vaterland*), a short drama which he also wrote and directed (both films 1911).[67]

In particular, Qværnstrøm recognized the width of August Schønemann's abilities, even more so than any of the young actor's previous mentors. Haakon B. Nielson writes that Qværnstrøm «understood to place the ambitious young man [Schønemann] in roles suited to his talents.»[68]

Schønemann's contract at the Folk Theater paid him a monthly salary of 140 Crowns, the equivalent to a little over $1,000 today. A considerable paycheck for an aspiring actor at the time, Schønemann no more had to spend any wearisome hours within cramped store basements. Furthermore, he could refer to himself as a fulltime actor. It was during this period, at Qværnstrøm's Folk Theater, that the first true reviews of August Schønemann's stage achievements flourished. In one paper, even, his signing of the contract in October 1911 was treated with a brief notice.[69]

The ink on his new contract barely dry, August Schønemann once again embarked on tour. The Folk Theater had behind them a successful tour across the country the previous spring, staging such plays as the comedy *Baldevin's Marriage,* among others.[70] As the company undertook a new tour in the fall of 1911, Schønemann was assigned a supporting role. Then, in November, Ludvig Müller's 4-act play, *The New Sheriff,* was staged by the company, with Schønemann again playing a supporting role. Pehr Qværnstrøm himself played the leading role, as the Romani Franz impersonating (you guessed it!) a sheriff.

Notably, the author of *The New Sheriff* was son to one of Norway's most famous authors in history, Amalie Skram, but he never reached fame comparable to his mother. Even so, *The New Sheriff* was deemed a crowdpleaser in its day, with the Folk Theater's interpretation receiving at least one glowing review.[71]

Schønemann's engagement at the Folk Theater lasted until the spring of 1912. During his six-month period there, he was, to some degree, established as a *stage personality* to the public – still not a «star», but reviewers had definitely begun to take notice. The final play of the fall season, Wilhelm Winter's «detective comedy» *Det uhyggelige Portræt* (*«The Gruesome Portrait»*), was a big hit, as was the first play of the spring season, the 3-act comedy *Spøgelseshuset* (*«The Haunted House»*), also penned by Winter. In the latter, Schønemann received one of his first major roles, as one «rentier Silberstein».

For his next big role, Schønemann appeared as a «retired old man» in the comedy *Det gjør ingenting* («*It Doesn't Matter*»). Granted, one reviewer found the young man's appearance to be «at times too youthful» for this particular character.[72] On the other hand, reviewers noted no objections to his role as an unlucky barber in a farce entitled *Telegrammet* «*(The Telegram*»*)* by Georg Bernick; as the barber, Schønemann «appealed very much to the public's taste».[73]

Other plays staged by the Folk Theater in the spring of 1912 include (for the second time in Schønemann's career) *Jeppe on the Hill*, with Schønemann now playing a secretary; *Svigermor! Pas Paa!* («*Mother-In-Law! Be Careful!*»); *Hittebarnet* («*The Orphan*»); *Paa Dydens Vei* («*Virtue's Path*»); *Kvindelist* («*Cunning Women*»), in which Schønemann played a «very old lady»; and *Ægtemandens Representant* («*The Husband's Representative*»).

A few exceptions such as Holberg's *Jeppe* aside, most of these plays must be considered rather «plain» comedies. However, the company also experienced a triumph with a dramatic play entitled *Gold Diggers* (here referring to the actual, physical activity of gold-digging; the word doesn't really carry a «double meaning» in the Norwegian language, as is the case in American).[74] Schønemann seems not to have played a prominent role in this drama, though, if at all. His boss Qværnstrøm understood the young man's talents to be more suited to a comic context, and so he allowed Schønemann to instead perform solo gigs *prior* to each performance of *Gold Diggers*, in which the comedian made use of his «funniest jokes and newest songs».[75]

A 16-year old girl by the name of Kirsten Flagstad accompanied Schønemann on the piano during these solo gigs. A youth of considerable talent herself, Flagstad would, with time, evolve into Norway's greatest dramatic soprano, being one of few Norwegian performers in history to reach international fame. In one biography on Flagstad, the sophisticated teenager's choice of music, during these particular performances, is said to not have always been ideal, however – amidst the merriest of moments onstage, she could suddenly bring herself to play Beethoven's Sonata Pathétique![76]

(We'll get back to Schønemann's acquaintance with Flagstad a bit later in our story.)

The Folk Theater may have preferred to play in the «big cities», but Qværnstrøm was well aware of the steady thirst for entertainment among the rural population of Norway. However, touring an oblong country such as Norway, with its highly varied geography, proved a cumbersome task to practically any theater company that ever dared to try it. Even by the early 2000s, Norwegian performers have been known to dread touring certain remote parts of the country, so we can just imagine how performers felt about it a century earlier. Perhaps more often than not, actors and crew alike grew weary of both each other and themselves while on tour, but, as the saying goes, *the show must go on.* Furthermore, traveling theater troups were often forced to perform in less than ideal environments. Sometimes, the only available premises to hold performances included worn, wooden sheds in the country.

Still, to Qværnstrøm's troupe, it must've been of at least *some* consolation to discover that audiences greeted the ensemble with unreserved enthusiasm on nearly all occasions. Haakon B. Nielson recounts an amusing tale of the troup's visit to a remote village in the county of Oppland, in which they were scheduled to perform some breezy comedy. In the play, Schønemann appeared as the lover to an unfaithful wife, her furious husband played by Qværnstrøm. The scenario asked for a scene in which the «jealous» Qværnstrøm, in a fit of rage, was to frantically run towards August, and chase him around the stage. Surely these two (by now) professional actors should've been able to pull *this* scene off, under normal circumstances – but regrettably, the primitive stage on which the play was performed lacked facilities for such a «chase sequence». Schønemann solved the problem by rushing towards the edge of the stage as Qværnstrøm chased him, whereupon he did a formidable jump downwards and disappeared «beneath the proscenium.»[77]

By May 1912, August's memorable phase at the Folk Theater reached its conclusion, as the theater's operation ceased in its then-current form. The reason is unclear, but it seems not to have happened without notice. Happily, Pehr Qværnstrøm could still offer temporary jobs to most of his actors for the time being, Schønemann included. The month before, the troupe had signed a contract with the Summer theater of Kongsberg (yet another suburban town nearby Kristiania). Starting June 1 and lasting for three months, at the Summer theater the troupe performed a total of seven plays and operettas outdoors, no doubt to the delight of sunseeking audiences from nigh and afar. Comic songs were also part of the program.[78]

While this engagement no doubt provided a welcome paycheck during the summer months, the salary was nowhere near as decent as had been the case at Qværnstrøm's own Folk Theater. August received a «mere» 100 Crowns each month, and found himself expected to be available at the Summer Theater at all times throughout the engagement.[79] The plays performed at the Summer theater were largely restagings of the Folk Theater's greatest triumphs of the past year, such as *Baldevin's Marriage*. Some of their other plays that summer, such as *Andersen, Pettersen & Lundstrøm*, Schønemann had performed on previous occasions. A few dramatic plays were also staged at the Summer theater, including a 3-act play entitled *Guilty*, in which Schønemann received a major role as a district attorney. According to one review, for this role he received «all kinds of praise.»[80]

Throughout the spring and summer of 1912, Schønemann had dazzled audiences and reviewers alike onstage with increasing frequency, but whereas Hauk Aabel had served as the «big draw» at Fahlstrøm's Theater, Pehr Qværnstrøm himself remained the star of

Qværnstrøm's own acting troupe, both at the Folk Theater of Kristiania as well as the Summer theater at Kongsberg. Schønemann's roles had grown in size and importance, no doubt about it, but his true breakthrough remained on hold. To expect otherwise would, perhaps, have been unreasonable, especially if one considers that he was still only 21, having just reached the legal age of the time.

Still, he was far from an untried card anymore. August Schønemann possessed extraordinary talent, that much was clear to anyone who'd witnessed his performances.

Notes

55. Personal commentary in Aug. Schønemann's scrapbook: «*Obs! Jeg var ansat som suflør [sic] ved Fahlströms Theater fra 9 – August 1909 til Theatret opløstes den 30de August 1911.*» («NB! I was employed as prompter at Fahlstrøm's Theater from August 9, 1909 until the Theater was dissolved on August 30, 1911.»)

56. Nielson, p. 20.

57. *Morgenbladet*, March 10, 1910, p. 3.

58. *Fremtiden*, April 12, 1910, p. 3.

59. *Morgenbladet*, July 22, 1910, p. 3.

60. *Arbeiderbladet*, July 29, 1939, p. 8. Essay by Per Kvist.

61. Nielson, pp. 20-21.

62. *Trondhjems Adresseavis*, May 19, 1911, p. 2.

63. Nielson, p. 21.

64. Theater program + Schønemann's commentary in scrapbook, 1911. See also Nielson, pp. 21-22.

65. *Aftenposten*, morning edition, August 31, 1911, p. 1.

66. *Dagbladet*, September 28, 1911, p. 3.

67. Hansen, Halvard Normann: *En bok om film og kino ved Sarpsborg kommunale kinematografers 50-års jubileum* (Frank Vardings Trykkeri, Sarpsborg, 1965), p. 102.

68. Nielson, p. 22.

69. Newspaper notice stored in Schønemann's scrapbook, dated October 4, 1911 (paper unidientified, translated): «At Qværnstrøm's Folk Theater, gentlemen Olaf Wilhelms, previously employed at Fahlstrøm's Theater, and Aug. Schønemann, have [recently] been hired.»

70. *Dagbladet*, June 28, 1911, p. 2.

71. Nielson, p. 24 – cites review written by author Bernt Lie. Nielson's source unknown to me.

72. Newspaper notice, undated, in Schønemann's scrapbook.

73. Newspaper notice, undated, in Schønemann's scrapbook.

74. *Vestfold Arbeiderblad*, February 23, 1912, p. 2.

75. Nielson, p. 24 – cites newspaper ad, source unknown to me.

76. Rein, Aslaug: *Kirsten Flagstad* (Ernst G. Mortensens Forlag, 1967), p. 34.

77. Nielson, pp. 25-26.

78. Handwritten note in Schønemann's scrapbook: *«Da Folketheatret opløstes den 12. mai 1912 blev samtlige . . . engagerede til 'Kongsberg Sommertheater' for sommerens saison fra 1ste Juni til 1ste September.»* («When the Folk Theater was dissolved on May 12, 1912, everyone [from the troup] . . . were engaged at 'Kongsberg Summer Theater' for the summer season from June 1, to September 1 [, 1912].»)

79. Contract from the Summer theater, dated April 3, 1912, signed «August Schönemann», stored in Schønemann's scrapbook.

80. Newspaper notice, undated, in Schønemann's scrapbook.

Chapter 5

«TIVOLI» of Christiania Tivoli

Idle days seemed to lie ahead of Schønemann once again, as his engagement at the Summer theater of Kongsberg neared its concluding performances. (As his daughter was to point out more than sixty years later, when looking back upon *her own* career: «freelancing didn't really exist back then [prior to the mid-20th century]; any actor not tied to a theater was considered 'unemployed.'»[81]) Thankfully, yet another esteemed theater mentor happened to cross August Schønemann's path. While actor Paul Magnussen is nearly forgotten today, even in Norway, he was not an inconsiderable figure in the world of Norwegian theater in the early 1900s. Like Schønemann's earlier bosses Fahlstrøm and Qværnstrøm, Magnussen may be of importance to our story primarily due to his role as a sort of «mentor» to the comedian, but he certainly knew how to capture audiences in his own right. Moreover, Magnussen shared Schønemann's penchant for comedy, perhaps to an even greater degree than what had been the case with Fahlstrøm and Qværnstrøm. It's easy to imagine the two of them getting along quite smoothly. However, having lived a decade or so more than

Schønemann, Magnussen had made a name for himself in the business several years prior to their first encounter. By 1912, newspapers described him as a «nationally known» revue actor.[82]

Beyond such long-forgotten newspaper notices, Magnussen may today strike us as a somewhat mysterious figure, a performer about whom it's hard to find tangible information. (At the time of this writing, there appears to not even exist a brief Wikipedia article devoted to him online, not even in Norwegian. Although he enjoyed quite frequent publicity in the press up to his death in 1942,[83] his fame, sadly, has not endured.) It also remains largely unclear what kind of material Schønemann performed while under Magnussen's wings. Schønemann's handwritten notes indicate that he remained with Magnussen for about a year, from August 1912 to summer 1913,[84] but the absence of paper notices and theater ads is striking. Historian Haakon B. Nielson gives us no further clues about Schønemann's year with Magnussen, either. Based on paper ads which yours truly has seen, Magnussen primarily did comic sketches during these months, so we may assume that Schønemann served as a sort of «sidekick» to him onstage, as the two of them perhaps exchanged light banter with one another. Among other things, Magnussen, and probably also Schønemann, appeared at the Circus World Theater of Kristiania for several weeks in the spring of 1913.[85]

The name of Circus World Theater (Cirkus Verdensteater) may not ring any bells to many readers today, not even to people from Norway, but for years, this cylindrical building remained a crucial part of Kristiania city life, before its eventual demolition. Within the walls of this magnificent construction, August Schønemann was to return many a time.

Considering that Schønemann had been given opportunity to show his worth in leading roles the year before, he may have thought it a step backwards, in a sense, to suddenly serve as Magnussen's sidekick. To share the stage with the (for now) more famous

Magnussen no doubt offered valuable lessons to young Schønemann, lessons which he'd probably not want to be without, but as their partnership came to an end in mid-1913, he didn't hesitate to approach «old» Pehr Qværnstrøm once again – or, for all we know, Qværnstrøm may have sought out Schønemann first. Another summer was on the rise, the Summer theater of Kongsberg again stood at Qværnstrøm's disposal, and we can imagine a joyous occasion to have taken place as August was reunited with his old colleagues, for yet another sunny season outdoors.

Kirsten Flagstad (1895-1962) first met Schønemann at the age of 16, while providing piano accompaniment to Pehr Qværnstrøm's 'Folk Theater' troupe. With time, she'd evolve into a world-famous opera singer, and one of the most famous Norwegian women to have ever lived. Here seen as 'Elsa' in Wagner's 'Lohengrin' in 1915. (Nasjonalbiblioteket / The Norwegian National Library.)

Legend has it that 22-year old Schønemann got his first taste of love during this second stint at the Summer theater of Kongsberg. It's probably advisable to say «legend», as the author has not been able to verify the claim, although we can't rule it out entirely, either. As noted in Chapter 4, the later so famous Kirsten Flagstad had served as pianist to Qværnstrøm's acting troupe on previous occasions, and she had, as such, accompanied Schønemann's merry voice onstage many a time already. Even so, it was apparently during these summer months that the comedian's heart for her began to ponder. He is said to have behaved almost «scatterbrained» on their first performance together that season, to such a degree that even the public, apparently, was befuddled. However, as the inhabitants of Kongsberg, throughout these summer months of 1913, were to spot a young couple strolling «in moonlight along the country roads nearby, they came to understand why Schønemann had appeared so awkward at the premiére,» Nielson writes lyrically.[86]

It would be interesting to get a hint as to from where the story of Schønemann and Flagstad's romance originates. Schønemann barely touches his private life in his surviving scrapbook, so any comment from him on the matter has proved impossible to obtain. Even in the exstensive Flagstad-biography referred to in Chapter 4, we have to search in vain for any more information regarding the alleged romance. While doing research for his book on Norwegian revue in the 1960s, Haakon B. Nielson was able to interview certain people who knew Schønemann, and so he may have received information about the alleged Schønemann-Flagstad romance in that context, but again, we cannot say for sure. *If* a passionate relationship indeed took place between the two of them at one point, it cannot, at any rate, have lasted for very long. By 1913, Flagstad's own career was about to reach a turning point. Later that very year, she made her debut at the National Theater in Kristiania, and her world fame was soon a fact. In particular, Flagstad's rising star was to be promoted by a certain Hungarian theater director, a charismatic talent scout with whom we are soon to get better acquainted.

The sunny months at the Summer theater came to an end also this time around, but finding work was no more a burden to August Schønemann. By October 1913,[87] he could proudly proclaim to his parents that the popular stage of 'Tivoli Theater' (located right behind, but not in any way tied to, The National Theater) had gained new blood, with Schønemann expected to play alongside plenty of notable talents, such as the later so legendary Norwegian singer Victor Bernau (1890-1939).

Main entrance to the amusement area of Christiania Tivoli. While the 'Tivoli' was established in 1877, its iconic entrance was not completed until 1890. (Photo: Axel Lindahl. Wilse collection / Norwegian Museum of Cultural History.)

It is perhaps worth spending a minute or two explaining the term *tivoli*, since it reappears quite a few times in this book. Whereas today, the word is typically used in Norwegian to describe modern amusement parks, offering activities and facilities such as carousels, rollercoasters and «haunted houses», the term carried a broader meaning back in the early 20th century. Back then, a «tivoli» could also refer to a place for audiences to seek out comic theater, songs and sketches. As such, 'Tivoli Theater' constituted *one* of several «sections» at the large amusement area of *Christiania Tivoli* mentioned previously, which had its headquarters in the center of the city (any reader feeling a bit confused right now is entirely forgiven). As recounted above, Christiania Tivoli had first opened its doors in 1877, modeled after a similar amusement area in Copenhagen, Denmark, and for decades remained *the* place for joyful recreation in Norway's capital city.

Being one of the most popular venues of the large amusement area Christiania Tivoli, the building of 'Tivoli Theater' was a sight to behold, by the 1910s embellished with «Persian» onion domes atop each of its front corners. Here, Benno Singer's 'Theatre Moderne' operated from 1914 to 1925. This photo from the late 1920s. The building was finally torn down in 1937. (Photo: Ruth Raabe / Oslo Museum.) (This work is licensed under the Creative Commons Attribution-ShareAlike 4.0 International License. To view a copy of this license, visit http:// creativecommons.org/licenses/by-sa/4.0/ or send a letter to Creative Commons, PO Box 1866, Mountain View, CA 94042, USA.)

Actually, 'Tivoli Theater' had roots as far back as the 1830s,[88] but was heavily renovated upon the construction of Christiania Tivoli in 1877. By the time August Schønemann entered its stage for the first time in 1913, the place had been further modernized (and was to be refurbished yet again the following year, as we shall see in the next chapter). Indeed, the building of 'Tivoli Theater' became a sight to behold, embellished with «Persian» onion domes atop each of its front corners, making it perhaps the most easily identifiable venue of the large amusement area.

Once employed at Tivoli Theater of Christiania Tivoli, Schønemann made sure to note in his scrapbook that he'd done «great success» playing the tailor 'Bodin' in the French stage comedy, *73 Champignol* by Georges Feydeau & Maurice Desvallières,[89] despite the fact that his role in the play accorded him only a single line, one friend remembered.[90] During the same period, he also appeared as a «stenographer» in American Bayard Veiller's drama, *Within the Law*, as well as a 3-act comedy entitled *Lys over land* (*«Light Across Land»*), written by celebrated Norwegian poet Herman Wildenvey (d. 1959).

1913 had stood as a landmark year to August Schønemann. Having appeared alongside renowned actor Paul Magnussen onstage, and just recently joined the popular hall of Tivoli Theater at Christiania Tivoli, he must've discerned the contours of a breakthrough not far ahead of him. Sadly, the year was to end on a somber note, as his father, August Pettersen Sr., passed away eleven days before Christmas Eve, at the age of 68. The funeral took place at the Chapel of Sofienberg Graveyard (today demolished since long ago).[91]

Came spring 1914, his engagement at Tivoli Theater also concluded, for the time being.[92] Happily, Schønemann's comic partner of the year before again embraced the young actor with open arms. Paul Magnussen handed Schønemann a big role in an

«Anniversary Revue» at Tivolihagen – an outdoor facility for summer entertainment at Christiania Tivoli – from July 16,[93] celebrating the centenary of the Norwegian Constitution. However, although by all accounts a great success in the «Anniversary Revue», Schønemann was to receive a more lukewarm response as he went on tour with Magnussen in the fall, at least initially. Appearing at «Varden Market» in the county of Telemark, Schønemann performed a comic song satirizing the riots and cases of hoarding which had swept over Norway (like many other countries), following the outbreak of World War I in the summer. Apparently, the audience didn't much care for the satire, for reasons unknown – they may've hoped to spend the evening without being reminded of the war, or perhaps they recognized themselves all too well in the lyrics which Schønemann brought to life onstage through his cheerful voice. Whatever the reason, the lack of applause puzzled Schønemann a great deal, according to fellow actor Karl Pedersen. By now, Schønemann had reached a point where he could count on the public's enthusiasm whenever he entered a stage.[94]

We may assume that the song was dropped from subsequent performances, for the press notices of Schønemann's tour with Magnussen that fall are almost unanimous in their praise: appearing in the town of Rjukan in October, Schønemann was found to «sing really well», his «mimicry» declared «superb».[95]

Above all else, however, during Schønemann's initial period at Tivoli Theater in 1913—1914, yet another «mentor» had caught an interest in our actor, perhaps the single most important person of August Schønemann's career: a charismatic impresario by the name of Benno Singer.

Notes

81.   Radio interview with Aud Schønemann. NRK. June 1979.

82. *Fremtiden*, April 19, 1913, p. 3.

83. *Sandefjords Dagblad*, June 15, 1942: «Actor Paul Magnussen is dead in Oslo at 60 years of age.»

84. Nielson, p. 28, + handwritten note in Schønemann's scrapbook.

85. Various papers of the time, such as *Fremtiden*, April 19 and 25, 1913.

86. Nielson, p. 33.

87. Nielson claims that Schønemann was employed at Tivoli theater in August 1913 (p. 28), whereas Schønemann's notes in the scrapbook state October 1913 – an agreement for him to appear there may have been made in the late summer, whereas his performances may have commenced in the fall.

88. Then known as 'Klingenberg Festsal' («Klingenberg Hall»).

89. Handwritten notes + theater program in Schønemann's scrapbook.

90. *Humør 1932* (Bernau, Victor), pp. 138-139.

91. Obituary notice, *Aftenposten*, morning edition, December 17, 1913, p. 8 (translated): *". . . Artisan and Decorator August Pettersen (previously in the firm R. Ramberg & Co.) died today 68 ½ Years. Kr.a. 13/12 – 13 . . ."*

92. Probably in April or May. Schønemann's scrapbook.

93. Madsen, Birger: *Arbeiderforeningens Teater – Tivoli og Tivoli-Haven, Lokal Teaterhistorie 1875-1939* (Næsgaards Boktrykkeri, 1975), pp. 88–89.

94. Ibid.

95. *Rjukan*, October 10, 1914, p. 2.

Chapter 6

Futt

A native of Hungary, Bernhard Henry «Benno» Singer was of Jewish descent, but his family had immigrated to London when he was a child, in the 1880s. Once there, he found himself part of various theater activities from an early age, and proved to possess talent as organizer in that regard. He's likely to have been inspired by certain legendary impresarios in Britain of the time, such as Charlie Chaplin's great «mentor», Fred Karno.

With time, Singer moved to Norway, probably not expecting to stay for long, but the possibilities of theater operation were more promising in the country than he'd perhaps imagined. The population may have been small in size – less than 2.4 million in 1910 – but with more free time given to most ordinary workers from the late 1800s forward (the 10-hour work day had been introduced in 1897), a thirst for entertainment thrived among the population just the same.

World Exhibitions became one of Singer's «specialties.» In Norway, he is today chiefly remembered for having organized part of the famous Centennial Exhibition at the Frogner Park of Kristiania in 1914, celebrating the 100th anniversary of the country's Constitution. (It should also be noted that Singer's display of so-called «ethnological expositions» at the Centennial Exhibition that year makes him a problematic figure in our times.)

Singer, reportedly, never really learned to speak Norwegian, beyond a few words, but he made himself reasonably well understood through an Hungarian-accented English from his boyhood years.[96]

Following his role during the Exhibition at the Frogner Park in 1914, Singer initiated a renovation of the amusement area of Christiania Tivoli. Despite its ongoing popularity with the public, the operation of Christiania Tivoli had not been the story of an unmitigated success, as it had struggled to cover its expenses ever since the Kristiania stock market crash of 1899. By the time Singer entered the scene, the «Tivoli» had, in fact, ceased to manage circuses and playhouses in its own right, confining its focus to the operation of restaurants and motion-picture screenings while renting out premises to private theater companies, who paid their own expenses. However, determined that the potential of Christiania Tivoli was not all spent yet, Singer had new theaters opened on the lot from 1914 onwards, launching a renaissance for the amusement quarter which was to last for roughly about a decade.

A perhaps not entirely sympathetic caricature of theater directors Bernhard Henry 'Benno' Singer and Alexander Varnay, early 1920s. Artist: Fredrik Christian Bødtker. (Oslo Museum.)

According to Haakon B. Nielson, a contract between Schønemann and Singer was signed in the late summer of that year.[97] Yours truly has been unable to track down any such contract between the two of them, as it appears to be absent even in Schønemann's scrapbook (in which most of the actor's contracts remain stored to this day). It's entirely possible that an agreement was made between the two men that month, but in general, Singer must have found himself preoccupied with the Centennial Exhibition – which lasted until October that year – as well as the completion of his new variety theater, «Theatre Moderne», whose lights first glimmered the following month. Occupying the aforementioned building of Tivoli Teater at Christiania Tivoli, the interior of Singer's «Theatre Moderne» had undergone a considerable renovation before its grand opening (in the summer months, it was to offer performances outdoors in the years ahead). One paper announced on November 20, 1914:

Theatre Moderne

The new variety theater of our city opens its doors this evening. Under manager [Benno] Singer's magic wand stands now a magnificent theater hall in white and purple, blessed with a great lighting system, and comfortably heated; the old area surrounding the building is barely recognizable.

Theatre Moderne is to be a variety theater of British fashion, [with] just two long breaks . . . Mr. Singer has wished to create a light and pleasant theater, where husband and wife, and also the children . . . can expect to spend a joyous evening, and at this he has succeeded.[98]

Only inches away, in the very same paper, news of the ongoing Great War were outlined, which by now had reached its third month (and was not known as the «Great War» yet). Norway's status as a neutral country notwithstanding, also there the need for merriment may have seemed especially crucial now.

At the onset, Theatre Moderne kept itself occupied staging one-shot variety performances, in other words comic sketches and routines which were not part of a «revue», per se. As far as the author can tell, Schønemann was not seen onstage during its first few months of operation, at least not in any large role. We do not know the reason to this, and it seems indeed curious, especially given Haakon B. Nielson's statement that Schønemann had signed a contract with Singer months before. In part, the comedian may have been affected by the loss of his second parent at this time. Thrine Josefine Pettersen, b. Engebretsen, had died unexpectedly in the night of October 16, 1914, ten months after her husband, at the age of 63.[99] The grief must have been considerable to Schønemann. He was, after all, still only in his early twenties, an early age to have lost both parents, also back then. Other than himself, only his sisters Agnes, Anna and Berthe Marie remained of the close family by now.

Fortunately, he did not lack prospects, and probably managed to not let himself be overwhelmed with gloom. As the holidays approached, he found himself preoccupied with rehearsals to the first big revue of Theatre Moderne: Thorleif Klausen and Michael Flagstad's *Futt*.

An informal Norwegian word to describe high levels of energy, *Futt* was to achieve a legendary status in retrospect. «Everyone» who'd attended it appeared to remember it fondly, for years afterwards. Its prémere held on Thursday, February 18, 1915,[100] the show was to be staged «Every Evening at 8» o'clock in the weeks ahead, treating the public to «10 first-rate Variety installments.»[101] Schønemann was to mesmerize audiences in no less than *three* separate roles this time, including the leading role of an insufferable professor named Jo Vellesen, as well as a «cop» and, finally, a frostbitten soldier on duty at the «Oscarsborg

Fortress» of Norway. The play's co-author, Thorleif Klausen, recalled that Schønemann had not been expected to play more than one role in the revue initially, but «as rehearsals progressed, he undertook one role after the other, demonstrating his unquestionable talent for all of us to see, to the point where he, in the end, *became* the whole revue.»[102]

Benno Singer's Theatre Moderne, which from 1914 to 1925 occupied the building of Tivoli Theater. Here from the theater's summer stage, 1914. (Nasjonalbiblioteket / The Norwegian National Library.)

In particular, it was for his role as the «frostbitten soldier», or *neutrality guard*, that Schønemann made an unforgettable impact. Whenever retrospective articles on Schønemann were penned in later years, it was often for his portrayal of *this* character that no amount of superlatives seemed to do the comedian full justice. Perhaps this could partly be attributed to the fact that Schønemann, with this role, expressed something vital about his contemporary times, an important reminder of life *there and then* in the year of 1915 – admittedly in the guise of delightful comedy. As noted above, Norway remained «neutral» throughout World War I, but this is not to say that the horrors of the war passed the country by like a gentle breeze. To the contrary, maintaining a «neutral» position proved tough on the country's resources, a fact which Norway's underprioritized armed forces witnessed firsthand. Germany declared the entire North Sea for war territory, and so each time acts of war took place nearby, Norway had to react soberly – any signals liable to be interpreted as favoritism, in one direction or the other, had to be avoided at all costs. Nonetheless, about 1,200 Norwegian sailors are reported to have died in shipwreck during these years, as a direct result of the war.

August Schønemann as the 'Neutrality guard' in the revue Futt *(1915), the role that made him a national star. Signed photograph. (Nasjonalbiblioteket / The Norwegian National Library.)*

Hence it was decided, at the Fortress of Oscarsborg – a coastal fortress opened in the 1850s and used for military purposes for the next 150 years – to have soldiers serve as so-called *neutrality guards*, a formidably hard duty to perform during winter months.

Dressed in a pile of garments, wool scarf and earmuffs, poor «neutrality guard» August Schønemann thus found himself marching back and forth onstage, deeply «frostbitten», while performing his little song on *Neutralitetsværnet («The Neutrality Defense»)*. A satisfying translation of the lyrics in English is nigh on impossible to achieve, relying as they do on Norwegian slang and phrases, but yours truly has done his best here:

Dengang jeg dro avste'

i slaps og sludd og sne,

da tenkte jeg som så,

nå fryser du deg blå.

The day I was bestowed

my spot in slush an' snow,

I wasn't slow to reckon,

I'd turn to ice in a second.

Men selv om du får gikt,

så husk det er din plikt,

D' er nok av dem som her

vil bryte sitt gevær.

But though I've developed gout,

I ain't got a single doubt.

While some may dream of desertion,

toward those I feel aversion.

Når Drøbaks samlag står,

så trur jeg nok det går.

Det blir en ferietur,

om kanskje litt vel sur,

men det gjør ikke no'

når labskausen er go'.

The kinship of Drøbak will thrive,

an' so we shall survive.

It's basically a vacation,

albeit at a chilly location.

My complaints remain quite few,

I've got a bowl of ample stew.

[Chorus:]

For ut på Oscarsborg ved juleti'

der gives ingen sorg, der er jeg fri.

Når kona ellers tar og slår meg gul,

nøytral hu' holdt seg – nå siste jul.

At the Fortress I spend the yuletide,

with prospects mighty 'n wide.

While the wife's known to be brutal

This year she stayed – quite neutral. . . .[103]

The song, popularly known as *Oscarsborg ved juleti'* (*«Chris'm's at Oscarsborg»*), was written by Klausen, and became a smash hit (by the standards of the day; of course, radio broadcasting was not yet a thing). It's unfortunate that no recording seems to have been made with Schønemann's interpretation of the song. It is, however, easy to imagine how he performed it, and why it turned out such a success, when one listens to other songs recorded by him later on. Always eager to hear audiences roar ever more, Schønemann no doubt performed the song with slight variations from one performance to the next, and likely found time to adlib a quip or two during performances (consider, for instance, the brief «pause» in the final line of the first chorus). Although Schønemann very rarely «wrote» his own material, per se (at least not as far as the revues are concerned—it's likely that some of his comic monologues during solo performances were his own), he attained the reputation of a clever adlibber, who could not be relied on to strictly follow a script. Legend has it that the author to one of Schønemann's many revues dropped by Theatre Moderne one night to see the revue he'd penned be performed, some six weeks after its premiére, as he'd not before had a chance to witness it come alive in person. Reportedly, Schønemann's adlibs were so numerous that the revue's author found it necessary to buy a program sheet, to assure himself that the theater indeed *was* performing the revue he'd written.[104]

Ordinary audiences were not alone in finding *Futt* a scream. Reviewers, too, found much to praise in *Futt*, with *Dagbladet* («Norw. *Daily News»*) describing the revue as «a tremendous triumph night after night. Having been sold out each night since the premiére, new details are frequently added to the show. The lovely adornments of the auditorium also receive . . . great applause.»[105]

Although in retrospect, it's clear that *Futt* marked the big *breakthrough* of August Schønemann as a stage personality, it may not at first have been evident to Theatre Moderne, or Benno Singer, that this was to be the case. Initially, reviewers were somewhat slow to mention Schønemann by name, although there could be no doubt that he, as the *neutrality guard*, portrayed one of the most «memorable characters» of the revue.[106] Despite Singer's obvious faith in the comedian, Schønemann seems not to have been promoted as the «star» of *Futt* from the getgo. He was, after all, still relatively unknown to the public at large, but as the weeks progressed, more and more reviewers made a point of singling out his performances – and from now on, Schønemann did not have to hunt for *local* newspapers to see his name in print. Stills of him dressed as the frozen guard soon appeared in nationwide press.

Caricature of Schønemann as the 'Neutrality guard.' 1915. (Nasjonalbiblioteket / The Norwegian National Library.)

It goes without saying that a success of *Futt's* caliber could not have its lifespan confined to a single stage in Kristiania. Although the capital city offered the largest amount of potential audiences, word of the great revue spread across the country. By late April, inhabitants of the towns Moss and Fredrikstad could also savor the big show.[107] Granted, the local paper of the latter town labeled the revue's content as «somewhat thin», but this was made up for by its many memorable performances, with «August Schønemann» generating «the greatest ovations».[108]

In the second largest city of Norway, Bergen, *Futt* was performed at the Concert Hall (Konsert-Paleet) in May, several days in a row.[109] By New Year of 1916, it was estimated that Schønemann had played the revue to a packed house at least «130 times».

Schønemann's newfound fame may at first have puzzled the man who, by one account, was known among friends as «the most modest soul one could imagine.»[110] Initially, he also seems to have struggled to separate himself from the pitiful «neutrality guard» with whom the public had grown so fond.[111] His friend and fellow actor Ragnvald Wingar, who'd known Schønemann since his days as prompter at Fahlstrøm's theater, recalled an evening where the new star confessed to feel almost «eaten up» by the character: «I can't sleep at night until I've placed my army boots in the closet, and hung my leg warmers by the bedpost.»[112] Although probably uttered partly in jest, the statement must nonetheless have expressed something vital about his new life. Says Haakon B. Nielson: Schønemann «so much immersed himself in his performances, that he became one with the characters he portrayed.»[113]

As summer of 1915 approached, 24-year old August Schønemann found himself one of the most celebrated comedic talents of Norway.

Notes

96. Various authors: *Humør 1932* (Aschehoug, 1932), p. 135. Essay on August
     Schønemann by Kvist, Per.

97. Nielson, p. 29.

98. *Middagsavisen*, November 20, 1914, p. 3.

99. *Dagbladet*, October 16, 1914, p. 2. Obituary notice (translated): *"Widow Thrine Josefine Pettersen 63 years 9 months."* See also *Aftenposten*, October 19, 1914 ("...died suddenly last night").

100. *Social-Demokraten*, February 18, 1915, p. 5.

101. *Aftenposten*, evening edition, February 22, 1915, p. 6.

102. *Humør 1932* (Kvist, Per), p. 133.

103. Original Norwegian lyrics cited in Nielson, pp. 30-31 + Kvist, Per, pp. 133-134. Attempt at English translation by yours truly.

104. *Teaterkattens 25aars Jubilæumshefte*, 1923, p. 48.

105. *Dagbladet*, February 26, 1915, p. 3.

106. *Morgenbladet*, April 11, 1915, p. 2.

107. *Moss Tilskuer*, April 17, 1915, p. 2.

108. *Fredrikstad blad*, April 19, 1915, notice from Schønemann's scrapbook.

109. *Bergens Tidende*, May 6, 1915, p. 3.

110. *A-Magasinet*, June 16, 1927, p. 11.

111. Paper notice from Schønemann's scrapbook, paper unidentified but dated March 1, 1916.

112. Nielson, pp. 31-32.

113. Ibid.

Chapter 7

A Chaplinesque Kick in the Belly

Actor Paul Magnussen, who'd served as Schønemann's employer just two years prior, was understandably impressed by the younger comedian's recent accomplishments. By late spring 1915, Schønemann had already become a well-established presence at Benno Singer's Theatre Moderne – and would remain so in the years to come – but as summer approached, Magnussen leapt at the chance to resume contact with the new star. Magnussen was eager to engage Schønemann for another «Summer theater», this time to be held in the town of Fredrikstad; and Schønemann gladly accepted the offer, along with the rest of Theatre Moderne's talented acting crew.[114] Schønemann primarily appeared onstage on Wednesdays and Thursdays in these months,[115] in addition to various stand-alone performances. Not surprisingly, he frequently reappeared as the «Neutrality guard» on these occasions.

Much pleased with the results, Magnussen did not wish to let go of Schønemann and the rest of the crew, as summer 1915 drew its last breath. Determined to go on tour, he convinced Schønemann and other crew members to let themselves be «borrowed» from

Theatre Moderne, so that Magnussen could stage his own version of *Futt* across the country. With this in mind, a contract was signed between Schønemann and Magnussen on August 15, which was declared valid «from the date in September 1915 that the tour begins, to the day when Schönemann is required to begin [new] rehearsals at 'Theatre Moderne' . . .»[116] Schønemann's salary was to be 350 Crowns a month (the equivalent to about $2,000 today; for a Norwegian actor of the time, this was considerable dough). Similar contracts (by now lost) were made with other important members from the original staging of *Futt*, including well-known Danish actress Asta Nielsen.[117] The tour of Magnussen's *Futt* took off in Fredrikstad, the town in which the same crew had appeared during the bygone summer. Beginning in early September, Magnussen's take on *Futt* was deemed «one of the better performances to have been staged» in the town.[118] The entire crew was said to do their roles well, and «once Schønemann entered, we had for sure arrived at the highpoint» of the evening.[119]

Following their success in Fredrikstad, the ensemble appeared in the counties of Ringerike, Grimstad and Møre-Romsdal up to late October.[120] Whereas August Schønemann had turned into the most popular comedian of Kristiania in the spring, he now also conquered the hearts and minds of the country at large.

All success across the nation notwithstanding, Schønemann still appears to have felt a particular devotion to Benno Singer's Theatre Moderne. It was, after all, while under Singer's supervision that he'd first achieved broad fame. Other theater managers would entice the comedian with tempting offers, from time to time, but for the next eight years, Schønemann nearly always found time to appear at Theatre Moderne. From a financial standpoint, Singer probably benefited the most from Schønemann's loyalty, more than the comedian did himself – but even so, it may have been a wise decision for Schønemann to prioritize Theatre Moderne to the degree that he did. Following a couple more revues there, he evolved into a sort of «mascot» to the theater.

Now and then, however, Schønemann apparently dared to ask Singer for a raise. On one such instance, he's said to have made light of Singer's characteristic language, a combination of Hungarian, English and (to a small degree) Norwegian: «Ein kleines Vorschuss, Mr. Director,» Schønemann reportedly quipped; «What do you say to dass?»[121] (The latter word is Norwegian slang for toilet. It's obviously impossible to verify some of the «amusing tales» which surround the legend of August Schønemann, but the author will include some of them in the book, while reminding readers that certain anecdotes may have been embellished with time.)

Expectedly, once Paul Magnussen's take on *Futt* completed its run in the fall, Schønemann returned to Theatre Moderne. On November 16, 1915, another revue had its première at the theater, by the name of *Sort paa hvidt* (*Black on White*), a.k.a. *Kristiania Mosaik*. While this revue did not, in retrospect, attain a legendary status comparable to that of *Futt*, the new revue was greeted with similar zest at the time. «[Benno] Singer has not held back on the equipment,» one paper declared; «there was a rich display of sparkling colors, exquisite color effects», etc. However, more than color effects and decorations, the success of a revue relied on the talent of its performers, the same reviewer conceded, and Norway was «not known to be well-heeled in this regard, but [actors] Erling Holck, Pehr Qværnstrøm, [and] Schønemann . . . made a great impression and provided some fine characters. . . .»[122] (Pehr Qværnstrøm had evidently joined Theatre Moderne.)

The female players impressed this particular reviewer less, but then again, this had just been opening night. The *Black on White* revue underwent significant changes in succeeding weeks, more so than what had been the case with *Futt*. Some actors were discharged and replaced, while new sketches and characters were added throughout the revue's time. Schønemann remained for the whole run, of course, once again repeating the song of the poor *Neutrality guard*, among other things. Danish actress Asta Nielsen went along with this revue as well, although offers from other, more prestigious theaters were numerous by this time. Perhaps most notably, in *Black on White*, a certain Swedish performer by the name of Ernst Rolf (briefly mentioned in Chapter 2) also appeared, to the great excitement of audiences. We shall get to know Rolf better later on in the book.

It's worth noting that some forward-thinking souls arranged to have excerpts from this revue recorded and released on gramophone. Unfortunately, the author has not found any copy of the record, and does not know if it's at all possible to obtain at this point, but it generated big advertisements in the Norw. *Evening Post* throughout the winter of 1916.[123] The record was distributed by the company of Skandinavisk Grammophon.

Black on White enjoyed a three-month run at Theatre Moderne, until February 1916. As it reached its end, actor Paul Magnussen was again allowed to stage his own version of Theatre Moderne's popular revue elsewhere, among other places at the newly-established Victoria Theater in Karl Johans gt. (Kristiania),[124] although this time, Magnussen lacked one important ingredient to the show. Schønemann seems not to have joined him this time, busy as he was with rehearsals to the upcoming *third* revue at Theatre Moderne. A revue by the name of *Razzia* was then staged in March, 1916 at Singer's theater,[125] and, if we are to believe a caricature printed in the humor magazine of *Tyrihans*, Schønemann here appeared in a sketch parodying none other than Charlie Chaplin.[126] Chaplin had, of course, at this time just recently achieved world fame (his first film having been released in the States two years prior, at least one newspaper ad confirms that Chaplin's films had reached Norway no later than February 1915, with a screening of the one-reel film *Laughing Gas*). Granted, Schønemann himself did not himself appear as the great Chaplin (an actor named Josef Sjøgren did), but according to the aforementined caricature, Schønemann *does* seem to have received a heavy kick in the belly from «Chaplin»!

Caricature of actor Josef Sjøgren as 'Charlie Chaplin,' giving Schønemann a heavy kick in the belly in the revue Razzia *at Theatre Moderne. March 1916. (Nasjonalbiblioteket / The Norwegian National Library.)*

As with Theatre Moderne's previous revue, new sketches and characters were added to *Razzia* throughout its run. Although well-received on the whole, this revue lasted for a bit briefer than *Futt* and *Black on White*, until the end of April,[127] after which Theatre Moderne's program was reserved for one-shot variety numbers for a while to come. No new revue was in store for the remainder of the spring; most likely, the crew, and perhaps Benno Singer himself, found it necessary to recover from an extremely busy season, but Theatre Moderne still continued to harvest vast numbers of audiences, providing the public with various singers, dancers, magicians and comedians in standalone performances, performers from foreign countries as well as Norway. Of course, reviewers were not always appreciative – for some reason, the Norw. *Evening Post* often appeared particularly hard to please – but most of Theatre Moderne's shows seemed to include at least *one* sketch, or song, that made it time well spent after all.

A number of waiters were needed at the theater, mostly to pour beverage to audiences;[128] in spite of (or perhaps, partly *because* of) the liquor ban which had been introduced in the country that year (although initially motivated by a poor supply situation due to the War, moral and social grounds were also cited by opponents of liquor sale).[129] Schønemann kept busy doing an assortment of one-shot performances throughout the late spring of 1916. A solo gig held on Midsummer's night (June 23) that year accorded him great publicity.[130]

By late summer, Schønemann again teamed up with Paul Magnussen, this time at Folkets Hus (The People's Hall) in Kristiania, re-performing the most memorable songs of the earlier *Black on White*-revue.[131] Surely it must've been a great joy to Schønemann to now receive star billing alongside his old mentor. Once again, Magnussen convinced the comedian to go along on tour, which this time took off on August 20,[132] to do a revue entitled the *Farris Tour*[133] (referring to a famous Norwegian lake). With a schedule nearly identical to their tour together of the previous year, Schønemann, Magnussen and the other crew members now visited the towns of Fredrikstad and Moss, among other places.

The *Farris Tour* of fall 1916 marked a temporary break from Theatre Moderne for Schønemann. In addition to the revue with Magnussen, he spent these months doing several more standalone gigs, also under Magnussen's supervision.[134] We can hope that he, at least, found time for a day off on Saturday, November 18, 1916 – incidentally the last day of the Battle of Somme – when his sister, 29-year old Berthe Marie, went to the altar with 26-year old storeclerk Thorleif Nielsen (we may also hope that the newlyweds weren't *too* much bothered by the fact that they both got their names spelled wrong in the marriage register, see footnote).[135] The marriage was celebrated in a villa at the Eastern part of Kristiania.[136] For the next several years, Berthe was to serve as a trusted secretary at Theatre Moderne.[137] Like her brother, she was to adopt the surname of «Schønemann» for the rest of her life. While she has been described as «the very antithesis to her famous brother, with her . . . sense of strict diligence»,[138] her colleagues also described her with terms such as «loving» and «extraordinarily esteemed».

Newspapers noted the name of AUG. SCHØNEMANN with increasing frequency towards the end of 1916, in letters bolder than before. However, he still found himself only at the inception of his popular breakthrough.

Notes

114. *Smaalenes Social-Demokrat*, September 1, 1915, p. 4.

115. See, for instance, *Smaalenes Social-Demokrat*, August 11, 1915, p. 3.

116. Handwritten contract stored in Schønemann's scrapbook, dated August 15, 1915, signed Paul Magnussen.

117. Asta Nielsen (1881-1972) enjoyed a long, fruitful career in theater and film alike. One of her most memorable achievements includes an appearance in G. W. Pabst's film, *Die freudlose Gasse* (1925) with Greta Garbo.

118. *Smaalenes Social-Demokrat*, September 2, 1915, p. 3.

119. Ibid.

120. *Ringerikes Blad*, September 25, 1915, p. 3; *Grimstad Adressetidende*, October 2, 1915, p. 3; *Romsdals Amtstidende*, October 18, 1915, p. 3.

121. *Humør 1932* (Kvist, Per), p. 135.

122. *Middagsavisen*, November 17, 1915, p. 3.

123. *Aftenposten*, evening edition, February 18, 1916, p. 2.

124. *Daggry*, March 4, 1916, p. 3.

125. *Aftenposten*, morning edition, March 16, 1916, p. 8.

126. *Tyrihans*, February 1916. Found in Schønemann's scrapbook.

127. *Norske Intelligenssedler*, April 11, 1916, p. 6 (translated): *"The revue 'Razzia' at Theatre Moderne is played only for one more week...."*

128. Various job ads for Theatre Moderne seeking waiters, *Aftenposten* 1916.

129. The 'Norwegian Prohibition' was repealed in 1927.

130. *Aftenposten*, morning edition, June 22, 1916, p. 4 + *Morgenbladet*, June 23, 1916, p. 5.

131. *Akershus Social-Demokrat*, August 5, 1916, p. 3.

132. *Akershus Social-Demokrat*, August 5, 1916, p. 2.

133. *Smaalenes Social-Demokrat*, August 14, 1916, p. 5.

134. See, for instance, *Smaalenes Social-Demokrat*, November 9, 1916, p. 5.

135. Marriages: 1916-11-18. Church book from Jacob parish 1908-1922 (0301M7). (SAO, Jakob prestekontor Kirkebøker, SAO/A-10850/F/Fa/L0010Parish register (official) no. 10, 1908-1922, p. 81.) Note: «Nielsen» gets spelled «Nilsen» in the marriage certificate, but other records on Thorleif's family in church books confirm that «Nielsen» was generally used (see, for instance, Census 1910 for 0301 Kristiania kjøpstad: Thorleif Nielsen, b. 1890-05-20). Berthe is, on her part, given the surname «Schønemann Petersen», single *t*, and her deceased father August Pettersen is also listed as «Petersen». Again, it bears mentioning that most people weren't too nitpicky

about the spelling of names 'back in the day,' although it's still perhaps a bit surprising in this case.

136. *Akers-Posten*, November 18, 1916, p. 2. Berthe's surname also gets misspelled here ('Petersen'), although they get Thorleif's right.

137. *Arbeiderbladet*, October 8, 1947, p. 2.

138. Gulbrandsen, Lars O.: *Aud Schønemann – Det blir mellom oss* (Se og Hør Forlaget, 1997), p. 27.

Chapter 8

"Seven Roles Tonight"

New Year of 1917 gave Norway some fiercely cold winter months. The country suffered from coal shortage, due to Britain's cancellation of coal supply to Norway with the aim of halting the Norwegian export of minerals to Germany. Schools had to be closed for long stretches due to the shortage. Be that as it may, the need for fun and recreation persisted. Radio broadcasting belonged to the future, so in order to experience performances, families of Kristiania had to grit their teeth and bravely embark on a frozen expedition, out to the various playhouses which the city could provide. For Schønemann, the year took off with a guest appearance at the Herdahl Salon of Kongsvinger on January 5.[139] Being part of the Skiing Association's Fair (*Skiforeningens marked*), the performance was repeated several evenings in a row.

By mid-January, the time again came for the comedian to appear at Theatre Moderne, casting him in a brand new variety program. A reviewer in the Norw. *Evening Post* did not express great enthusiasm this time around, though, stating bluntly that he'd found both Schønemann and the other players «funnier in previous shows».[140]

This slight disappointment notwithstanding, as a venue of popular entertainment, Theatre Moderne now enjoyed its golden era. If one considers not only the revues staged there throughout 1917, but also their many standalone performances, the theater's schedule that year becomes too vast to summarize in its entirety. In addition to the various cabarets staged there, aimed at a more mature audience, humorous sketches with children and youths in mind were also frequently performed.

Actor and writer Thorleif Klausen (1882-1934), who wrote the majority of Schønemann's revues at Theatre Moderne, and appeared with him onstage on a number of occasions. Here from a stage appearance in 1909. (Oslo Museum.)

At the so-called «Sunday matinees», staged at Theatre Moderne and other theaters, Schønemann evoked perhaps most acclaim of all. For a single such performance, lasting about twenty minutes, the comedian now received at least 250 Crowns[141] (equivalent to about $1,060 per 2021). It may have been chiefly as a *revue performer* that Schønemann secured for himself a «place in history» – but it was, perhaps, at the more intimate matinees that he left the greatest impression on the citizens of Kristiania, during his own lifetime. For sure, stage life provided its share of obstacles – quite often, he was obliged to perform three times in one day, such as at a matinee arranged on May 17 this year (Norway's national day), at one, five and finally eight o'clock P.M.[142] – but the public could always rely on his good spirits, as he greeted them with indestructible humor and warmth.

However, impresario Benno Singer was well aware that *revues* generated the most publicity to his costly variety theater, more so than the many one-shot performances, and by October 1917, another big show was ripe for premiére at Theatre Moderne. Given the somewhat «Biblical» title of *Mammon*, the new revue was once again penned by Thorleif Klausen, co-author of the theater's first success *Futt*. Of course, Klausen had written the revue with the purpose of, hopefully, evoking laughter among the public, but one reviewer remarked that the revue could also be viewed as «a slice of real life», as it apparently took inspiration from certain «dark tendencies» of the time,[143] suggesting elements of satire in the show. This seems indeed to have been the case; in *Mammon*, Thorleif Klausen very likely intended to put into question the ethics of the Norwegian war profiteers of 1915—1916. As World War I had reached its most deadly phase for the soldiers in the trenches, Norwegian shipowners and stock market speculators enjoyed a period of astounding prosperity. Although the Norwegian government was met with intense pressure, from multiple quarters, to assure that the nation *must* maintain its neutrality in the war, plenty of desired items from

Norway, such as fish, continued to reach German borders (causing Britain to cancel its coal supply to the country, as noted at the beginning of the chapter). The Norwegian prime minister of the time, Gunnar Knudsen, wished as far as possible to avoid governmental intervention for private industries, and so, for a time, Norway became a leading creditor nation. However, this economic «golden age» came to an abrupt end soon enough, causing multiple bankruptcies and a severe economic crisis in Norway.[144] In the revue *Mammon*, the controversy surrounding Norwegian war profiteering was cleverly embodied through August Schønemann, as he appeared in the role of a young messenger boy who, following a series of hurdles, wound up a millionaire shipowner – only to lose his entire fortune in the end, poorer than ever before. In the role, he again affirmed his position as «one of our most gifted revue players», one reviewer stated; public applause forced him to re-enter the stage «several times» after the show's conclusion on opening night.[145]

Caricature of Schønemann as sudden shipowner 'Peter Michelsen' in the revue Mammon *at Theatre Moderne, 1917. (Author's collection.)*

Divided over three acts, the revue also provided a parody on *Carmen*, no doubt inspired by the new tour of *Carmen* which the aging mezzosopran, Gina Oselio, undertook on the grand stages of Norway at that time, having played the role numerous times since she appeared as the country's first «Carmen» in the 1880s. In addition, spectators of *Mammon* were treated with a ballet, starring a 21-year old dancer known as Kitty Normann (b. Kitty Benedikte Pedersen), a woman with whom Schønemann was soon to become better acquainted. In the end, *Mammon* was staged a total of sixty times within two months, always to a «crowded house».[146]

By early 1918, Schønemann was again asked to perform at the cylindrical playhouse of Circus World Theater in Kristiania, where he'd performed as actor Paul Magnussen's sidekick back in 1913. He appeared in various matinees at the theater throughout January, joined by *Mammon* ballet dancer Kitty Normann.[147] However, Benno Singer was of course eager to have the comedian star in a fresh «New Year's revue» at Theatre Moderne, entitled *Dusch*; and so it came to be, with Schønemann now portraying a suffering cop «who can't write a ticket to a car or arrest a drunken fella from the nearby bar»[148] (a comic phrase which, no doubt, had the Great War in mind – sale of gasoline to private automobiles had become temporarily banned, due to inflation – as well as the aforementioned Norwegian Prohibition).

The Great War neared its end, but no one were in a position to tell exactly when peace might become a fact. The war still had consequences even to neutral countries, Norway included. Ration cards for bread, flour, and coffee was now obligatory.[149] With many of the country's citizens being overwhelmed with frustration, the crime rate increased in this period. (Obviously, Norway was still better off with regards to the war than the countries directly involved in it.)

As *Dusch* reached its final performance after about a two-month run, Schønemann's professional life again consisted of standalone variety numbers, for the most part held at Theatre Moderne and the Circus World Theater,[150] after which another great tour awaited him, the comedian having decided to «embark on a journey around the [Norwegian] coast», once again in the company of Kitty Normann, as well as pianist Wilhelm Thorne.[151] Although the tour lasted for only ten days, they managed to drop by at least five destinations, including the relatively large cities of Bergen and Stavanger.[152]

Cirkus Verdensteater ('Circus World Theater'), another venue of Christiania Tivoli at which Schønemann appeared with frequency. The building, built in 'Renaissance Revival' fashion, was inaugurated in 1890, and housed a number of traveling circuses until 1908, after which it primarily screened motion-pictures along with live dance and song performances. It was torn down in the mid-1930s, along with the rest of Christiania Tivoli. Here photographed after a fire, 1910s. (Nasjonalbiblioteket / The Norwegian National Library.)

The little trio was then scheduled to do a number of fall performances at the Circus World Theater, but this had to be postponed due to a fire at the theater in the late summer.[153] Instead, Schønemann, Normann and Thorne undertook yet *another* tour across the country; in the town of Tønsberg, the trio's arrival was celebrated in the press with a portrait of Kitty, who by now found herself promoted as a star in her own right.[154] Although not yet 22 years old, she'd already become a dancer of considerable experience, and was promoted as such.[155]

Kitty Normann (1896-1989). January 1918. (Photo: Gustav Borgen / Norwegian Museum of Cultural History.)

Exactly when Schønemann's feelings for Kitty first blossomed – or her feelings for *him* – is not known, but we may assume it to have happened partly as a result of their many tours together (if love had not served as the primary reason behind their decision to go on tour together to begin with, that is). As early as a couple of years prior, a caricature of the two could be spotted in a humor magazine, in which they'd actually been described as «engaged» – a rumor which, predictably, was picked up by the Norw. *Daily News156* – although according to revue expert Haakon B. Nielson, their supposed «engagement» was only intended as a «joke» at that time.[157] Be that as it may, by fall 1918, genuine love seems to have evolved between the two of them.

Norway may not have been as severely affected by the Great War as many other European countries, but the infamous «Spanish flu» was to put a damper on theater life, from the first case of infection was discovered in the country in June 1918, and all the more so in the ensuing fall and winter. In Norway, an estimated 13 – 15.000 people died of the virus in the end, about 0.6 percent of the population, a rate nearly as high as in the States, and higher than Denmark and Germany. Schools were closed for long stretches at a time, and the same was true for several stage and movie theaters. Notably, Benno Singer's Theatre Moderne seems not to have shut down, even though audience attendance was clearly more limited during this phase. In the fall of 1918, the revue of *Hei paa dig* (*Hello to You*) was staged at the theater, but this time, Schønemann did not participate. He was, however, engaged by «Randall's Cabaret Company» to go on tour once more, heading up north to the county of Finnmark, again in the company of Kitty. With the pandemic in mind, Schønemann may have felt safer up north in the country. After one performance during this tour, a reviewer stated that «none of the younger comedians have probably ever conquered the hearts of the public on such a scale, as Schønemann . . . the appearance of his mere name on a program [is] sufficient for a show to get sold out.» It was stressed that, by now, Schønemann's songs were written with the comedian «specifically in mind», by «the best songwriters» that Norway could offer.[158]

Once the renovation of the Circus World Theater (following the fire in August 1918) was completed, Schønemann and Kitty Normann's postponed performances could finally be held there; this time, they were accompanied by Russian opera singer Michael Gitowsky.[159] During the holidays, they also played at the Park Theater of the Grünerløkka area, a few stone's throws away from Schønemann's first home address as a child.[160]

World War I was now over, Germany having capitulated and Emperor Wilhelm II abdicated. At the time, no one could've foreseen that the Emperor, known for his frequent visits to Norway before the war, in a way was to be «seen» onstage in Kristiania a few years later, as portrayed by August Schønemann.

***

Joining Schønemann in the «New Year's Revue» of 1919 at Theatre Moderne, was a young actress named Signe Heide Steen,[161] wife of tenor Harald Steen and, in later years, grandmother of beloved Norwegian comedian Harald Heide Steen, Jr (d. 2008). Carrying the title of *Paa stedet hvil* (*At Ease!*), the new revue was once again the brainchild of Thorleif Klausen, and starred Schønemann in the role of a frightened soldier on duty, apparently being spooked by witches and other supernatural creatures. It proved yet another smash hit to Theatre Moderne. By the end of its run in late April,[162] a revue called *Caviar* had already found its way to the theater, with Schønemann playing the double role of a piccolo and hotel director, as well as parodying some of his comic colleagues and even conducting the orchestra on occasion. He again played opposite Signe Heide-Steen, among numerous other notable talents.[163]

Schønemann's work capacity seemed boundless. He'd become a phenomenon across the country, and Kristiania in particular. Asked how he coped with such (by Norwegian standards) massive fame, he responded candidly that it «of course . . . can be fun, but not solely so.» He continued: «When, for instance, I find myself walking down the street with a 'swarm' of twenty urchins following me, as they whistle my latest tunes and yell, 'There's our August!' – No, that ain't no fun.» In fairness, some of Schønemann's other remarks in the interview suggest that he may not have been entirely serious on this occasion. When the reporter asked him if he could not, perhaps, at least *try* to stay serious for a moment during the interview, Schønemann responded that a «comedian can never be serious, and as a mime, my renown is so vast, that I am forced to lie with two rocks on each cheek at night, so that my face won't have an eruption.»

The reporter probably having a number of unanswered questions left in his notepad, Schønemann suddenly brought their conversation to an abrupt end, as he, by his own account, had to prepare for «seven roles» onstage that night.[164]

Notes

139. *Hedemarkens Amtstidende*, January 4, 1917, p. 3.

140. *Aftenposten*, morning edition, January 17, 1917, p. 5.

141. Nielson, p. 36.

142. *Dagbladet*, May 17, 1917, p. 5.

143. *Social-Demokraten*, October 17, 1917, p. 4.

144. Jensen, Magnus: *Norges historie – Fra 1905 til våre dager* (Universitetsforlaget, 1965), pp. 26—52.

145. *Social-Demokraten*, October 17, 1917, p. 4.

146. *Dagbladet*, December 14, 1917, p. 7.

147. *Aftenposten*, evening edition, January 11, 1918, p. 5.

148. *Aftenposten*, evening edition, January 2, 1918, p. 5.

149. Randen, Olav: *Brøyte seg til rydning – Bureisingstid og bureisarliv* (Boksmia forlag, 2002), p. 50.

150. *Social-Demokraten*, May 11, 1918, p. 8.

151. *1ste Mai*, May 28, 1918, p. 5.

152. *Stavanger Aftenblad*, June 3, 1918, p. 8; *Bergens Tidende*, June 6, 1918, p. 3.

153. *1ste Mai*, August 5, 1918, p. 2.

154. *Tønsbergs Blad*, August 15, 1918, p. 2.

155. *1ste Mai*, June 4, 1918, p. 1.

156. *Dagbladet*, August 1, 1916, p. 3.

157. Nielson, p. 36.

158. *Vestfinmarkens Socialdemokrat*, September 23, 1918, p. 2.

159. *Social-Demokraten*, November 22, 1918, p. 8.

160. *Social-Demokraten*, December 28, 1918, p. 7.

161. *Dagbladet*, January 8, 1919, p. 5.

162. *Middagsavisen*, April 19, 1919, p. 3.

163. *Middagsavisen*, March 14, 1919, p. 3.

164. *Nationen*, March 29, 1919, p. 3.

Chapter 9

Casino

By summer 1919, a puppet theater was ready to open its doors amidst the large area of Christiania Tivoli, named Tanagra (likely inspired by the Greek town of the same name, which was known for its terracotta figurines in ancient times). As anyone might expect, Schønemann appeared at the premiére performance on the new stage.[165] As fall arrived, he did another matinee at the Park Theater nearby his childhood quarters of Grünerløkka.[166]

For the fall season of 1919 at Theatre Moderne, however, Schønemann was teamed up with Danish-German actor Max Hansen in the revue *Dit og Dat («This and That»)*, consisting of «six installments» divided over «two acts».[167] With its premiére held on November 1 and once again written by Thorleif Klausen, *This and That* assured Theatre Moderne packed audiences yet again. Good chemistry was not lacking between Schønemann and co-star Max Hansen; Hansen, much later to become a star of film musicals in Scandinavia, seems to have gotten along swell with his (in a Norwegian context) more famous co-star of the show. Indeed, the two men welcomed the opportunity to appear together again in a matinee by New Year of 1920,[168] as well as other engagements.[169]

Two "elderly" fellows, as portrayed by the, in reality, considerably younger August Schønemann and Max Hansen. Most likely from the revue Paa'n igjen *('Here We Go Again') at Theatre Moderne (considering that the photo's date is given as 1920), but it may also be from the revue* Dit og dat *('This and That'), fall 1919. (Photo: Ernest Rude / Oslo Museum.)*

More revues starring Schønemann were on the horizon at Theatre Moderne during the first few months of the new decade, including *Tak! i lige maade!* (*Thanks, Same to You!*) in February[170] and *Paa'n igjen* (*Here We Go Again*) in April.[171] Perhaps most notably, also in April, he again appeared in a staging of *Charley's Aunt*, the play that had given him a first taste of (local) fame thirteen years prior – by now, he *certainly* did the starring role.[172] The play also seems to have been staged that year at the Summer theater of Fredrikstad, where he played alongside a young actress named Tore Segelcke – relatively unknown at the time, but soon to be a highly celebrated stage actress in the nation. She was not entirely pleased with Schønemann's «method», however. By now a star performer with a justified amount of self-esteem, Schønemann didn't feel any obligation to follow Brandon Thomas' famous play to the letter, which puzzled the more classically oriented Segelcke. Performing the play, Schønemann would adlib something new practically every night, to the delight of audiences and *most* of his co-stars, Segelcke being a notable exception. «How could such a renowned actor play around with the words [in the script], and just change any line as he saw fit?», Segelcke's later biographer asked rhetorically.[173]

A few exceptions such as Segelcke aside, Norway's delight in Schønemann's wild whims onstage remained pretty unanimous. Also in the summer of 1920, citizens of Trondheim, farther north in the country, were thrilled to make their reacquaintance with the star.[174]

His various engagements throughout the year being, again, too numerous to list in their entirety, the most notable event to occur in Schønemann's life in 1920 was of a more private nature. The paper *Nationen* announced in late August that «dancer Kitty Normann and actor Aug. Schønemann» were to get married, with their «wedding celebrated» on Friday, September 3 at Hotel Continental in Stortingsgt. of central Kristiania.[175] (The wedding ceremony seems to have been kept private. It's perhaps worth noting that the couple is named, in the marriage register, as «August Pettersen (Schónemann)» and «Kitty Benedikte Pedersen (Normann)», respectively.[176])

Our knowledge of August Schønemann and Kitty Normann's marriage is scarce, beyond the basic facts. As noted above, the couple had appeared together for (possibly) the first time three years before, in the revue *Mammon* in 1917, and their acquaintance may have gone even further back in time, if rumors of their brief «engagement» in 1916 are at all to be believed. Although their professional relationship had endured almost up to the wedding night, they seem to have reached an agreement that spending life onstage together may prove challenging now that they'd given their vows. For her part, Kitty largely kept herself occupied giving dance lessons at the

Hotel Bristol of Kristiania in the months and, eventually, years ahead.[177]

By the time of their marriage, Schønemann had moved into a comfortable apartment at Frognerveien 10,[178] and can, as such, be said to have left the relatively modest neighborhood of his upbringing behind him, «Frogner» being one of the more affluent areas to live in 1920s Kristiania (and remains so, in 2020s Oslo). Kitty was, for her part, still registered as living with her father at the time («expeditor Anton Pedersen»[179]), at Ullevålsvn. 85,[180] a distance of about 1.3 miles from the Frogner area, although it's safe to assume that she spent much of her free time at Schønemann's apartment, at least during this initial phase of their union.

Schønemann as 'tailor M. F. Traadsby' ('Threadtown') in the revue Overalls *at Theatre Moderne, performed November 1920 through February 1921. (Nasjonalbiblioteket / The Norwegian National Library.)*

The marriage did not compromise August Schønemann's career in any significant way. By early November, time had come for the premiére of yet another great fall revue at «the Moderne». Featuring a grandiose ballet number of at least eight dancers, the revue *Overalls* supplied Schønemann with a rather terrifyingly large pair of scissors onstage, as he enchanted audiences in the role of an eccentric tailor. The revue also paired him with a friend from his time at Fahlstrøm's Theater, actress Lilly Grimsgaard.[181]

Reportedly, *Overalls* marked writer Thorleif Klausen's «twelfth» revue at Theatre Moderne. In an interview conducted by the Norw. *Evening Post* to promote its premiére, Klausen described the opening night of a big show as comparable to a «lottery», but he also opined that he, as its writer, was «not the right man to ask.» Klausen insisted that a revue's writer is responsible for only «25 percent» of its success, while «the remaining three fourths» should be attributed to the work of the «conductor, decorative painters, ballet master, wardrobe inspector, the director, the prompter, the directorate, and the actors.»[182]

Although *Overalls* ran for seventeen weeks – through February 1921 – Schønemann and Grimsgaard also found time to appear at the Park Theater of Grünerløkka that fall, doing a play which may (or may *not*) have seemed particularly comic to newlywed Schønemann, a comedy entitled *Egteskap og Galskap* («*Marriage Madness*»).[183]

The lavish popularity of Theatre Moderne's revues notwithstanding, the theater also had to cope with harsh criticism from time to time. The revue *Galla Petter* («*White Tie Peter*»), first staged shortly after New Year 1921 and starring, yet again, Schønemann and Lilly Grimsgaard, was nearly panned by one critic. Although «Schønemann was given opportunity to shine as is his wont», even *he* came off as «somewhat tedious» this time around, the reviewer declared.[184]

In March, as Easter of 1921 approached, Schønemann and Lilly again starred together onstage, apparently for the last time, in the revue of *Snip, snap, snute*[185] – in which our hero, among other things, thrilled audiences with a sketch that had him «crossing the Atlantic» to seek the «Land of Opportunity», as several hundred thousands of Norwegian emigrants had done in preceeding decades (unlike these thousands of emigrants, however, Schønemann's «trip to the States» would remain confined to the stage of Theatre Moderne).

It may be worth pointing out that co-star Lilly Grimsgaard was to reach the ripe old age of 101; before her passing in 1994, she must have been one of the last persons alive to have starred alongside Schønemann onstage. Unfortunately, the author has found no proof that any interviews were done with her in later years, and does not, for that matter, know how her health may have been towards the end.

Although almost bombarded with lucrative offers from the many playhouses of Kristiania, Schønemann had remained loyal to Theatre Moderne for the past six years. He'd made sure to be at Benno Singer's service for nearly all of the theater's great revues since *Futt* in 1915. However, by spring 1921, a new chapter in his professional life was taking form. Following yet another string of performances at the Circus World Theater, as well as a few appearances outdoors in the town of Hønefoss,[186] perhaps even Schønemann himself came to realize that he had, in a sense, become «too big» for the intimate salon of Theatre Moderne. He may also, for personal reasons, have felt the need for a change of environment. Marriage with Kitty Normann had not turned out as expected. The couple made a guest appearance at the boulevard of Unter den Linden in Berlin during the summer,[187] but on October 6, 1921, separation papers were signed between the two of them, only thirteen months after the wedding had taken place (the couple remained formally married until fall 1923, however).[188] The couple may have discovered that sharing life together, day after day in an apartment in Kristiania, marked a stark contrast to the excitement of touring the country as performers, but this is speculation. Understandably, the two seem not to have appeared together onstage again, either. As far as the author can tell, the separation did not receive any attention in the papers – probably because no one tipped off the press – so the couple was at least spared from the many gossip and scandal columns of the day.

***

Casino theater – backstory summary

Ever since the inauguration of Theatre Moderne in 1914, Benno Singer had remained restless, feeling that his ambitions for Kristiania's theater life were still unfulfilled. Furthermore, he was no doubt dismayed when, in 1916, the City Council of Kristiania had decided that the area of Christiania Tivoli was to be «redeveloped», to make room for a new City Hall. Although the plans of the new City Hall, in the end, would remain on hold until the 1930s, assuring Singer several more fruitful years at Christiania Tivoli, he nonetheless began to seek out additional projects for himself. In 1918, he'd received permission to «borrow» the recently-constructed building of Stortingsgt. 16 to open yet another theater venue, which was given the name of Opera Comique. A «proper» theater housed in a modern, four-story building (plus roof on top), with four large, curved doors for its entrance, the building of Opera Comique had been financed by cinema founder Andreas Kvinnsland, sharing quarters with the supreme legislative building of Norway («Stortinget») across the street. An acquaintance of Singer's, Alexander Várnay, served as «head director» and CEO. It's worth noting that Opera Comique was meant to serve as only a «temporary» solution, initially, as the city awaited the construction of a grand «public opera» financed by shipowner Christoffer Hannevig – but plans of this «grand opera» had to be shelved in the end, as Hannevig declared bankruptcy shortly thereafter. Thus, for three important years (1918—1921), Opera Comique functioned as the first independent opera scene in the country. To put things in perspective: during Opera Comique's lifetime, the orchestra of Norway's National Theater had recently been reduced to a mere five musicians, whereas Opera Comique, meanwhile, could offer solists, a choir of 50 people, 20 ballet dancers, and an orchestra of 36. Although just a brief walk away from Theatre Moderne, Opera Comique enjoyed the reputation of a more «prestigious» stage than Theatre Moderne ever was. During its existence, the classics of Saint-Säens, Wagner, and others found their way onto Opera Comique's programs, and helped turn Schønemann's former sweetheart, soprano Kirsten Flagstad, into a major star.

At Stortingsgt. 16 of central Kristiania, Benno Singer's Opera Comique staged numerous classic operas and plays in the years 1918—1921. Only months after its shutdown, the venue was reopened in the fall of 1921 as Casino, a theater which made its mark staging more lighthearted plays and operettas. At Casino, Schønemann was hired from the getgo, with the play 'Damen paa Nr. 23' ('The Woman at Room 23'), and would remain there until 1924. Excerpt of photograph. (Nasjonalbiblioteket / The Norwegian National Library.)

By spring 1921, after three years of operation, Opera Comique shut its doors for good, largely due to disappointing audience attendance following the economic crisis in Norway of 1920—1921.[189] However, the venue was to be reopened that very fall as the theater of 'Casino', also under Singer's leadership.

And so, still before his separation from Kitty Normann was a fact, in the summer of 1921, Schønemann had agreed to appear in Casino's preliminary play, its premiére planned for early fall. The comedian would certainly not be on his own at Casino. In addition to Singer's presence, revue author Thorleif Klausen was to serve as Casino's CEO.[190]

Around the time of Casino's opening, Theatre Moderne ceased to operate as a revue theater, confining its program to standalone variety numbers (although this was not to last for long, as we shall see).

If there were still some «respectable citizens» of Kristiania around who'd never set foot inside the hall of Theatre Moderne, out of fear that their peers might think «badly» of them, these souls could now also enjoy the stage presence of August Schønemann without worry. Casino was a «respectable» theater by any standard. It's worth noting, however, that whereas Schønemann had consistently received top-billing in the revues at Theatre Moderne for the past several years, during his initial phase at Casino he was to appear chiefly in memorable, but somewhat smaller comic roles, while «starring roles» would be handed to more conventional leading actors.

The new theater's name apparently given as the result of a name contest,[191] Casino's grand opening took place on September 10, 1921 – not with a «revue», but rather a farce play by the name of *Damen paa Nr. 23* («*The Woman at Room 23*»). Set in a French garrison town,[192] the play starred actress Borghild Lyche as «the woman at room 23», whose attraction to men in uniform «forces her» to betray her husband, even though she «so very much» wishes to be faithful.[193] Schønemann served as comic relief, whereas the male leading role was given to Conrad Arnesen. Benno Singer and his crew may have taken for granted that they had a hit on their hands; in addition to Schønemann and Arnesen, old pro's such as Thorleif Klausen and Signe Heide-Steen appeared in notable roles. It's unlikely that anyone had questioned their chemistry during rehearsals.

'Leading man' Conrad Arnesen (1891-1955), who played alongside Schønemann in several operettas and plays at Casino in 1921—1924, as well as in the film Kjærlighet på Pinde (1922). (Photo: Thorleif Wardenær / Oslo Museum.) (This work is licensed under the Creative Commons Attribution-ShareAlike 4.0 International License. To view a copy of this license, visit http://creativecommons.org/licenses/by-sa/4.0/ or send a letter to Creative Commons, PO Box 1866, Mountain View, CA 94042, USA.)

Even so, on opening night, the lavish play *The Woman at Room 23* apparently fell like a stone, being arguably the first significant debacle of Schønemann's career since his breakthrough. «A decent farce must provide good lines and a tad of humanity,» complained the Norw. *Daily News*, «[but] *Woman at Room 23* . . . offered none of the above. The whole play consisted of one quite weak idea, tediously exploited within three long acts, material far too thin to entertain even the politest of Saturday spectators . . .» But whereas a few other reviewers claimed that even Schønemann came off as unremarkable this time around, the critic of the Norw. *Daily News* remained more understanding towards the star. The people in charge at Casino had simply picked a «weak play».[194]

Haakon B. Nielson writes that *The Woman at Room 23* was declared such a failure, that Casino found it necessary to cancel its run almost immediately, a claim repeated by yours truly in the original Norwegian edition of this book – but actually, critical failure or not, the play still ran for eight weeks, so the public at large may not have shared the critics' dismay to such a degree after all. Considering its painstaking promotion campaign on beforehand, though, the heads of Casino had likely hoped for a better critical reception.

Happily, the theater was to experience full restitution soon enough. The operetta of *En natt i Paradis* («*A Night in Paradise*»), which premiéred in October, was deemed such a success that Casino's next production had to be postponed for several weeks, due to public demand.[195] In this particular play, however, Schønemann did not participate, preoccupied as he still was with *The Woman at Room 23*. He was, on the other hand, to be seen in Casino's *third* big production, *Den evige lampe* («*The Eternal Lamp*»), starring older actor Fredrik Wingar while Schønemann, again, served as comic relief. Its premiére held on December 14, 1921, this 3-act farce ran for nearly three months.

As their first production of 1922, Casino staged French playwright Georges Feydeau's classic farce, *A Flea in Her Ear*, with Schønemann portraying hotel owner Feraillon, another noteworthy but smaller comic role.[196] Written at the height of La Belle Époque, and considered one of Feydeau's most well-known plays, with this comedy of mistaken identity, Casino were relieved to have yet another success on their hands.

The restaurant at Casino theater, c. 1920, where Schønemann spent many an evening in the early 1920s. (Photo: Anders Beer Wilse / Oslo Museum.)

Schønemann appears to have relished his time at Casino, becoming very much familiar not only with the stage there, but also the theater's popular restaurant. Legend has it that he, during one of his many visits at the restaurant, bumped into one Otto von Porat, who, despite his young age (reportedly just turned 18 at that point) had already made a name for himself as a professional boxer. Porat and Schønemann weighted «200 and 95 pounds, respectively,» Nielson writes. The two celebrities did not hold back on the beverage that night at the restaurant. Having treated themselves to all kinds of liquids and delicacies, time finally came for them to wander home, whereupon the peculiar duo could be spotted staggering along the crowded street outside. Out of the blue, reportedly, Schønemann then challenged Otto von Porat to a fight, his small fist flying towards the tall boxer's chin above him. Porat understood the joke, of course, and was not the least bit offended (or affected) by the comedian's modest uppercut – whereas Schønemann himself, however, appeared to be down-and-out as a result of his own punch, and «dropped dead» on the ground. Porat picked up the «unconscious» comedian from the ground, and had him thrown into a cab nearby.[197]

Perhaps embellished with time, if at all true, the story of Schønemann's encounter with boxer Otto von Porat merits a mention, as it evolved into one of the more well-known tales of the comedian offstage.

August Schønemann in private, at the height of his fame. Early 1920s. (Photo: Ernest Rude / Oslo Museum)

Whatever Schønemann may have thought or felt about his recent separation from Kitty Normann, we can only speculate about. Busy as he was, he may to a degree have managed to keep his mind off the more somber aspects of his private life. His first months at Casino initiated the very peak of his stardom, the relative disappointment of *The Woman at Room 23* notwithstanding.

Although we now, technically, have entered the decade later to be known as the «Roaring Twenties», in reality, life was of course as complicated as ever to most people. In Norway, the unemployment rate had reached huge numbers. Tens of thousands of people were without work, forcing municipalities around the country to implement emergency work. In 1921 alone, more than a thousand bankruptcies were registered in Norway. Even so, practically nothing could compare with the situation in Russia (which the upper part of Norway, of course, borders to), where horrible famine had spread across the country, mostly as a result of The Great War as well as instability following the revolutions of 1917. While not a particularly wealthy country at this point, also in Norway one felt an obligation to reach out a helping hand; and so, in late January 1922, an event was held at the concert hall of Gamle Logen, Kristiania, to raise «income for starving Russians.»[198] Initiated by a well-known theater director, the evening offered a «grand program» of numerous singers and actors, among them, not surprisingly, August Schønemann.

In many ways, though, the new decade may be said to represent a break from «old times», the dawn of a new era which, in essence, today may strike us as more recognizably «modern» than the decades preceeding it – a time during which much art, music, clothing and architecture was to challenge old boundaries. The «Victorian era», which could be said to have lasted for years after Queen Victoria's passing in 1901, had now definitely come to an end. These signs of a «new era» may have been more prominent in New York and Paris, but also in Kristiania, 1920s urban life made its mark on popular culture. In March 1922, Schønemann appeared in the revue of *Mr. Jazz* at Casino, which provided «twelve installments» divided over «three acts» including ballet numbers, and whose title, no doubt, referred to the new brand of «American music» which had been introduced as a term in Norwegian language just a couple of years before. Written by Klausen, the revue supposedly treated its spectators to a journey «across the globe», from Kristiania through India, to the North Pole and back again to Norway. It was deemed a «success», despite its «thin structure».[199]

"Fru Postmester" paa Casino.

Fra venstre: Aimarsen, Otti Pegel, Conrad Arnesen, Schønemann.

Caricature of Harald Aimarsen, Otti Pegel, Conrad Arnesen and Schønemann in the operetta Fru Postmester *('The Postmistress') at Casino. Aftenposten, May 1, 1922. (Author's collection.)*

The operetta *Fru Postmester* («*The Postmistress»*), with music by Polish composer Léol Jessel and starring celebrated Swedish opera singer Otti Pegel, was likewise declared a «fine and entertaining» play at Casino in the spring.[200] Once again, however, the male leading role was handed to the handsome Conrad Arnesen, with Schønemann doing a smaller part. This is not to say that Schønemann's performance was not duly noticed by the public or critics – to the contrary, as one reviewer pointed out, audiences burst out in violent laughter by the mere entrance of Schønemann onstage.[201] Regardless, to appear in smaller parts, in such tightly scripted comic plays, arguably provided Schønemann with less opportunity to showcase his versatility and ad-libbing gifts, no matter how «grand-looking» the productions at Casino were.

Arguably, it was with the «farce operetta» of *Reservebaronen* («*The Imaginary Baron*», German title «*Der Juxbaron*»), in the summer of 1922, that Schønemann was first given ample space to prove his worth at Casino. With music by famous German composer Walter Kollo, the play's world premiére had occurred in Hamburg in

1913, and turned into a sensation on numerous European stages in succeeding years. One of its most widely remembered tunes carries the name of «*Kleine Mädchen müssen schlafen geh'n*», with a verse going as follows:

Little girls must turn off the light
Once the stars stand in the sky at night.
An angel rocks her so gently and swell:
*'Good night, my darling, now sleep well!'*202

Schønemann (right) in the play Reservebaronen *('The Imaginary Baron'), one of his greatest successes at Casino theater. 1922. (Nasjonalbiblioteket / The Norwegian National Library.)*

Its Norwegian première held on June 5, 1922 at Casino,203 Schønemann's role in *The Imaginary Baron* would be remembered, in retrospect, as one of his most legendary figures, as he portrayed a «tramp» given the chance to pose as a «baron», a comic plot utilized in many plays, films and comic strips in the first few decades of the 1900s.[204] According to a critic of the Norw. *Daily News*, Schønemann was «solely responsible» for the play's success, its première performance constituting «the greatest opening night of any show we have seen this season, without question.» The reviewer predicted that the *The Imaginary Baron* would enjoy a «long life», which proved correct. Following its initial run at Casino in June, the play was staged several times at the Summer theater of Fredrikstad,[205] before returning to Casino for the fall season, as audiences simply would not tire of it. Its last performance was originally announced for February 18, 1923,[206] but public demand assured that it was still being played, at reduced prices, all the way through early April.[207] Indeed, with the *The Imaginary Baron*, Schønemann had made his quantum leap also as an actor of operettas. From now on, he would not, in the minds of the public, be so predominantly tied to the art of *revues* anymore.

More from Reservebaronen. *Schønemann to the far left. 1922. (Nasjonalbiblioteket / The Norwegian National Library.)*

By the early 1920s, the comedian's fame had reached such a level that «everyone» recognized him, also offstage. Some fans even dared to «wait» for him outside Casino around closing hours. «To take a walk in public with this popular folk hero was nigh on impossible», recalled his close friend, songwriter and fellow actor Vidar Wexelsen, better known by his pseudonym *Per Kvist*: «Within a few minutes, admirers of all ages swarmed around [Schønemann], and the lucky few who received a glance, or perhaps a remark from [his] lips, beamed with delight, as though they'd won the lottery.»[208] In nearly all of the many such situations which the comedian had to endure in the early 1920s, Schønemann seems to have greeted his fans with patience, but on one occasion, the crowd grew so intrusive that it became truly excruciating, Kvist reminisced. As Schønemann hissed to a particularly intolerable boy to get out of his way, the youngster was overcome with joy, according to Kvist: «Did ya hear that?» the boy yelled triumphantly, «August told *me* to get out of his way! *Me*!»[209]

Actor Per Kvist (1890-1947), one of Schønemann's closest friends. Early 1930s. (Photo: Unknown / Oslo Museum.)

Likewise, cab drivers are said to have «quarreled» (in friendly manner, one hopes) for Schønemann's attention, whenever the star sought a ride home from the theater at night.

Apparently, even the *law* was willing to accord Schønemann special treatment. Of all the legendary, «amusing tales» which surround the myth of August Schønemann, perhaps the most famous of all centers on a very late (or very early, depending on the perspective) nachspiel held in the morning hours of May 17, 1922, national day of Norway. Although inhabitants of Norway are not known to hold back on the celebration this day of the year (a hundred years ago as well as today), Schønemann can still be said to have «joined the party» a bit early when he, in the company of good friends, decided to start celebrating the evening *before*. Having stayed up all night partying in the first-floor apartment of (probably) fellow actor Fredrik Wingar at Grünerløkka, as the sun rose Schønemann got sight of a police officer outside, standing unsuspectingly below the apartment window. In a wink, Schønemann leaned out the window, pulled the officer's helmet swiftly inside, and disappeared behind the curtains. The officer rightly reckoned the thief's whereabouts to be in the apartment right behind him, and stormed inside the building in a flying rage. Once he'd entered the apartment, however, he was startled by the sight of Schønemann wearing his helmet, and reportedly burst out in a laughing stutter, «Oh, I could've sworn it was you all along, you nut . . . !» Apparently, the officer thought it a badge of honor to have his helmet stolen by the great August Schønemann, and so all was forgiven, no doubt to the relief of everyone attending the party.[210] Schønemann's friend and fellow actor, Einar Rose, recalled: «Schønemann was the only actor I knew who was equally hilarious *off*stage.»[211]

But although Schønemann's position as the Number One stage comedian of Norway was unquiestionable by this point, it must've been with mixed emotions that he, in the summer of 1922, undertook a first step into untried territory: to the world of *celluloid*.

Notes

165. *Dagbladet*, June 28, 1919, p. 4.

166. *Aftenposten*, morning edition, October 3, 1919, p. 7.

167. *Morgenbladet*, November 12, 1919, p. 3. In *Morgenbladet* of November 1, p. 2, it was said that the revue provided «eight installments» («*8 afdelinger*»), suggesting that a couple of installments may have been omitted from the revue after its initial one to two weeks.

168. *Social-Demokraten*, February 14, 1920, p. 8.

169. *Aftenposten*, evening edition, February 23, 1920, p. 6.

170. *Dagbladet*, March 6, 1920, p. 5.

171. *Nationen*, May 8, 1920, p. 3.

172. *Dagbladet*, April 17, 1920, p. 5.

173. Rønneberg, Anton: *Skuespillerinnen Tore Segelcke* (H. Aschehoug & Co., 1946), p. 24. Note: As far as yours truly can see, the Segelcke biography doesn't give an exact year for Schønemann's appearances with Segelcke in *Charley's Aunt* at the Summer theater of Fredrikstad. It most likely took place in 1920, however – given that Schønemann, as noted above, had already performed the play in April of that year, and Segelcke, still an unknown at the time, was to make her «big» debut the following year. Besides, as Segelcke was born in 1901, her participation in the play cannot reasonably have happened *much* earlier than said year.

174. *Trondhjems Adresseavis*, June 9, 1920, p. 3, + *Trondhjems Adresseavis*, July 15, 1920, p. 2.

175. *Nationen*, August 31, 1920, p. 2.

176. Parish register (official) for Uranienborg parish 1914-1930 (Oslo). (SAO, Uranienborg prestekontor Kirkebøker, SAO/A-10877/F/Fa/L0012Ministerialbok nr. 12, 1914-1930, p. 92.)

177. *Aftenposten*, morning edition, January 5, 1921, p. 7.

178. Parish register (official) for Uranienborg parish 1914-1930 (Oslo). (SAO, Uranienborg prestekontor Kirkebøker, SAO/A-10877/F/Fa/L0012Ministerialbok nr. 12, 1914-1930, p. 92.) Note: the building in which Schønemann lived in the early 1920s was torn down in the 1980s, replaced by an apartment complex in 1992/1993.

179. Church book from Nykirken parish 1926-1934. Marriages: 1931-10-17. (SAB, Nykirken Sokneprestembete, SAB/A-77101/H/Haa/L0038Parish register (official) no. D 8, 1926-1934, p. 103b-104a.)

180. Parish register (official) for Uranienborg parish 1914-1930 (Oslo). (SAO, Uranienborg prestekontor Kirkebøker, SAO/A-10877/F/Fa/L0012Ministerialbok nr. 12, 1914-1930, p. 92.)

181. *Social-Demokraten*, October 30, 1920, p. 4. See also *Aftenposten*, morning edition, October 14, 1920, p. 2.

182. *Aftenposten*, evening edition, November 1, 1920, p. 5.

183. *Social-Demokraten*, December 4, 1920, p. 7.

184. *Social-Demokraten*, January 3, 1921, p. 3.

185. *Social-Demokraten*, March 29, 1921, p. 4.

186. *Dagbladet*, May 26, 1921, p. 2.

187. *Aftenposten*, evening edition, July 23, 1921, p. 2.

188. August and Kitty were formally separated on October 6, 1921, and divorced September 9, 1923. From the archive of the County governor («Fylkesmannen») of Oslo and Akershus, marriage journal Fcc/1, journal no. 433/1921; as well as census card for deceased 1925.

189. Kindem, Ingeborg Eckhoff: *Den norske operas historie* (Ernst G. Mortensen – Forlagsavdelingen, 1941), p. 129.

190. Nielson, p. 37.

191. *Dagbladet*, August 16, 1921, p. 3.

192. *Dagbladet*, September 8, 1921, p. 6.

193. *Dagbladet*, September 12, 1921, p. 2.

194. Ibid.

195. *Nationen*, November 22, 1921, p. 3, + *Aftenposten*, morning edition, December 9, 1921, p. 9.

196. *Aftenposten*, morning edition, January 9, 1922, p. 3.

197. Nielson, pp. 49-50.

198. *Social-Demokraten*, January 27, 1922, p. 4.

199. *Den 17de Mai*, March 6, 1922, p. 4.

200. *Aftenposten*, morning edition, May 1, 1922, p. 5.

201. Ibid.

202. Ødegaard, Jac. R.: *Slagerboka – Populærmusikkens historie gjennom 200 år* (Tempo forlag A/S, 1953). p. 99. Fumbling attempt at translation of the verse by yours truly.

203. *Nationen*, June 3, 1922, p. 2.

204. See, for instance, Charlie Chaplin's two-reel films *Caught in a Cabaret* (1914), *A Jitney Elopement* (1915) and *The Count* (1916).

205. *Smaalenes Social-Demokrat*, July 24, 1922, p. 3.

206. *Tidens Tegn*, February 16, 1923, p. 10.

207. *Arbeiderbladet*, April 7, 1923, p. 9.

208. *Humør 1932* (Kvist, Per), pp. 148-149.

209. Ibid.

210. Rose, Einar: *Rose-boka* (Ernst G. Mortensen, 1941), pp. 33-34. Rose lets the owner of the apartment, where the prank supposedly took place, remain unnamed in his account, but Per Kvist identifies him as Wingar (*Arbeiderbladet*, July 29, 1939, p. 8).

211. Ibid.

Chapter 10

Silver Screen Stunts

One is tempted to ask, how did *seven long years* go by, from Schønemann's breakthrough in 1915, before anyone, apparently, had the stellar idea of assigning him a role in front of the camera? While today, we may view the «silent era» as a primitive phase in film history, in reality, motion-pictures had become a well-established pheonomenon, in the States and Europe alike, when the cameras first rolled on Schønemann's film *Kjærlighet paa Pinde* (literally means «*Love on a Stick*», but a more accurate translation would be «*Lollipop*»). Even back then, articles had begun to pop up in newspapers which looked back upon the first couple of decades of movie history with nostalgia.[212]

A difference between Hollywood and Norway in this regard is of course worth emphasizing. The production of Norwegian fiction films launched with the split-reel «*Fiskerlivets farer, et drama på havet*» («*Dangers in a Fisherman's Life, A Drama on the Sea*») around 1907–1908,[213] several more years were to pass before the country could offer anything resembling a *systematic* production of films. Even by the early 1920s, Norwegian film production was of a far more sparse nature than was the case in other Scandinavian countries. By contrast, in Denmark and Sweden, a «golden age» of film production arguably took place at this time, with such famous directors as Carl Th. Dreyer and Victor Sjöström.

However, modest though it may have been, *completely stagnant* the development of Norway's film industry was not. Between 1920–1922, at least eight feature-length films were produced, among them a dramatization of Knut Hamsun's classic novel, *Growth of the Soil*. On the other hand, attempts at *comic* films were nearly non-existent, the supply of film comedies being almost entirely confined to the jesters of France and the States: Max Linder, Chaplin, Harold Lloyd, Roscoe Arbuckle, etc. Granted, comedy production on film was not generally prioritized in Denmark and Sweden at the time, either, which is perhaps best exemplified by the fact that Sweden's «comedy king», Ernst Rolf, starred in only two film productions throughout the silent era.

Nonetheless, when time came to produce what resulted in the first Norwegian *film farce*, to be produced and distributed by Skandinavisk Film-Central and with Erling Eriksen and Leif Sinding at the forefront, it went without saying that August Schønemann had to receive a prominent role. Without permission from Casino theater, the film team «borrowed» Schønemann for a few weeks in the summer of 1922 (something Casino was *not* to take lightly, as we shall see), and managed to have the film shot within that limited timeframe, mostly outdoors, without attracting too much unwanted attention. By his own account, Eriksen covered all of the film's expenses himself.[214]

(The following may be of interest primarily to readers familiar with local Norwegian geography, but it's worth pointing out for accuracy's sake: in the original, Norwegian edition of this book, yours truly claimed that most of the film was probably shot at the municipality of Nesodden, and we are indeed told, through a title card in the film, that the main action takes place there. The author did find this a bit puzzling, however, since the smoothest way of transportation from Kristiania to Nesodden, by far, would be by boat, a journey which sounds needlessly burdensome to a 1920s film crew, considering that they had to drag along heavy film equipment, etc. It actually turns out that much of the film was shot in Kristiania, partly at director Eriksen's villa in the area of Nordstrand, as well as 'Vestre Aker prestegård' (Western Aker Manse).[215])

Erling Eriksen served as the film's director – for the first and only time in his career – and he is also believed to have outlined its «story», while Leif Sinding was assigned the role of scenographer and technical consultant.[216] Sinding's wife, 23-year old Ellen Sinding, made her screen debut as «leading lady», while opera singer Conrad Arnesen was hired as Schønemann's handsome «rival». Arnesen and Schønemann knew each other well by this point, having appeared together onstage on several occasions, including the critical failure of *The Woman at Room 23* at Casino the year before.

By Leif Sinding's account, the slim ambition had originally been to make a brief 1-reel film, in other words 10-15 minutes in length. He recalled that «Norwegian film, at that time, was trapped in a deep slope, and so the idea of a feature-length film didn't even occur to me … [I] suggested a brief short film similar to the treasured MacSennett [sic] farces.»[217] Even so, as their ideas multiplied during story sessions, the film crew finally wound up with a 4-reeler on their hands, nearly 45 minutes. As such, the finished film stands as rather ambitious in a Norwegian context. The crew must've been aware that a briefer, less costly film starring Schønemann would likely have generated nearly as many spectators. That they still went ahead with a 4-reel production, nearly a full-length feature at the time, is worthy of acclaim. The fact is that, in 1922, comic feature-length films had just recently begun to gain foothold even in the States. Up to the early 1920s, most people were of the opinion that «slapstick comedy» was unlikely to do well onscreen for more than half an hour or so. Granted, Frenchman Max Linder had made success with the one-hour *Le duel de Max* as early as 1913, and Mack Sennett's six-reeler *Tillie's Punctured Romance* became a smash hit soon thereafter, but these were considered exceptions. Other attempts at full-length «slapstick» on film did occur in succeeding years, but not until Charlie Chaplin's *The Kid* (1921) can we detect a true turning point in this regard. Chaplin's ability to blend slapstick humor with dramatic elements, which felt genuine and organic to the plot, had great impact on other comedians, and within the next two years, both Harold Lloyd and Buster Keaton abandoned production of short films in favor of features. Schønemann's screen debut can, in other words, be said to have happened almost concurrently with the *international quantum leap* of feature-length comedy films.

Artistic ambitions may not have been the foremost reason why *Kjærlighet paa Pinde* resulted in *four* reels of mayhem rather than a mere one reel, though. Perhaps more significant was the fact that the crew, reportedly, had an absolute blast shooting the film. By one retrospective account, performers and film crew alike found themselves practically «half-dead» in the evenings, caused by all the «laughing paroxysms» during each day's shooting.[218] Even a century later, it's not hard, as a viewer, to detect why the creation of this sunny production generated lots of fun memories to everyone involved. Whether the film which *resulted* from this merry shooting is entirely successful for that reason, can of course be debated, but more on that below.

Anyhow: the film, which, as noted above, is said to occur in the area of Fjellstrand, Nesodden, takes off with a title card, stating (translated): «*Fjeldstrand is an idyllic spot not far away from Kristiania, where a number of the city's prominent citizens have their summer villas. Here resides dancer Eva Sommer in her villa 'Flirtheim.'*» Immediately thereafter, another title card appears: «*Mr. Aleksander Snobman, a man of no past nor future, son of the most prominent supplier of knackwurst sausage in the city and himself a peculiar character, enjoys life in full at his villa 'Winterway.'*» And so he enters before us: August Schønemann in the role of «Aleksander Snobman», sitting at his balcony, derby on scalp, while ordering a maid to hand him his «medicine» for the day. (Audiences of 1922 would have recognized what kind of «type» Schønemann was here meant to portray, but it may be less evident to viewers of today: he plays a well-off, spoiled hypochondriac, a role that many another film comedian made use of on occasion, such as Harold Lloyd in *A Sailor-Made Man* (1921).)

In the next shot, we are presented to young Eva Sommer (Ellen Sinding) and her dog in their villa garden nearby, as they cheerfully inhale the rays of a sunny day.

His medicine devoured for the day, along with more than a tad of alcohol, «Aleksander» then decides to kill time by spying on neighbors through a telescope from his balcony. Soon enough, he gets sight of sweet «Eva Sommer», and is immediately smitten; he lets *«no chance of making her acquaintance pass him by»*, as a title card puts it. As the young woman later embarks on an evening stroll in the woods nearby, Aleksander eagerly approaches her in intimidating manner. She's not at all impressed with our «hero», and barely gives him a glance – whereupon he grabs her, and tries to kiss her by force (a scene which may not play so well to audiences of today). Fortunately, her screams for help are heard by another fellow nearby, the gentleman Philip Helt (Conrad Arnesen). Philip promptly comes to the rescue, and knocks Aleksander to the ground. She's accompanied home by her rescuer, who expresses understandable disgust with Aleksander's behavior. «Philip» and «Eva» are quite taken with each other, and agree to meet again the following day.

The rest of the film deals with Aleksander's hopeless attempts to outmatch his rival. Once he realizes Eva's passion for dancing, he's determined to become a dancer himself, and does an improvized dance number in «female» dancing clothes before us (still with derby on head). While on a drinking spree, he decides to challenge his enemy to a duel, sending Philip a mostly unreadable letter. One of the funniest moments of the film occurs when Aleksander arrives on the spot where the duel is to take place, rather nervously, and discovers to his relief that his rival is nowhere to be seen. He triumphantly concludes that Philip has not dared to show up, whereafter Philip, of course, turns up in full vigour. Philip has taken «Aleksander's» challenge quite lightly, however, so much so that he shows up with a gun made of chocolate.

Ellen Sinding, 'leading lady' in Kjærlighet paa Pinde *(1922), the only film in which Schønemann appeared. (Nasjonalbiblioteket / The Norwegian National Library.)*

When Aleksander later tries to knock Philip cold with a plank in the head while on the beach, he falls in the water himself instead, head first, and in the next scene, is seen with his entire head wrapped in bandages.

'Ballet dancer Snobman.' Schønemann in Kjærlighet paa Pinde (1922).
(Nasjonalbiblioteket / The Norwegian National Library.)

'Duel scene' from Kjærlighet paa Pinde (1922). (Nasjonalbiblioteket /
The Norwegian National Library.)

Towards the end of the farce, the filmmakers diverged from the main plot, as Eva and Philip decide to embark on a ride with an aeroplane, early 1920s model. For the next several minutes, we are treated with live pictures of Kristiania from high above, including the Norwegian Royal Palace and the area surrounding it. Spectators of 1922 must've found this scene a joy!

As summer nears its end, Philip graciously thanks Eva for her hospitality, and prepares for his return home. «Aleksander Snobman» is quite pleased to discover this, of course – finally, he's «rid of his arch enemy, and the hope that he may keep the lovely lady for his own lips swelled, with increasing passion, within him,» as one title card puts it. Of course, he's as unlucky as ever before. When a goat gets sight of «Aleksander» as he stalks the girl on the beach, he's quickly knocked off his feet, and lands head first in the ocean once more, whereupon he's attacked by an enormous crab.

Eva exclaims with laughter (in a title card): «Ha – ha – you may have had enough for now, Mr. Snobman, but we shall meet again in your next film!»

(As it turned out, the optimistic prediction at the end would not come true.)

One may well assume that the brains behind *Kjærlighet paa Pinde* didn't put overwhelming thought into the *plot* of this film. The main point was to get Schønemann in front of the camera; with him as ingredient, its success was a safe bet no matter what. From an aesthetic standpoint, the film nevertheless displays competent craftsmanship. The often idyllic surroundings of the actors are deftly captured, and the production remains quite pleasing to the eye. Photographer Erling R. Knudsen was to be rightly lauded in the press for his work on the film.[219] August Schønemann's character is pathetic and unlikeable, to be sure – a classic buffoon – but as a performer, the comedian manages to throw in lots of funny bits throughout, some of his facial gestures being hysterical in their own right. As with Chaplin, Schønemann's «smallest» gags are often the funniest, such as when he blushingly throws away his small parasol while on a stroll in the woods, after being called a «wimp» by the girl of his dreams.

Publicity shot from Kjærlighet paa Pinde *(1922). (Nasjonalbiblioteket / The Norwegian National Library.)*

Even so, there is no way *Kjærlighet paa Pinde* could encapsulate Schønemann's stage charisma and range. It seems obvious that he took the film less seriously than his major stage accomplishments. Also, if we allow ourselves to compare *Kjærlighet paa Pinde* with the feature-length films made by Chaplin, Harold Lloyd and, soon enough, Buster Keaton during the 1920s – as unreasonable as such a comparison may appear – it must be said that the film would've greatly benefited from a stronger intrigue. As any semblance of character development is absent throughout its duration, the film remains a thoroughly light affair, basically four reels of total nonsense. This, of course, would be fine for a 1- or 2-reel film, but once we're in near-feature territory, a certain amount of character development is usually to be recommended. (A similar distinction, interestingly, may also be applied when we compare *revue* characters and characters of *plays*; Schønemann's «Aleksander Snobman» would've worked flawlessly amidst a «revue sequence» onstage, no doubt, but probably less so as the main character of a *play*.)

Kjærlighet paa Pinde's status as the first film production of its kind in Norway, should again be emphasized. There's reason to believe that Schønemann himself would have gained greater influence behind the camera in succeeding films, had life gone differently for him. Another point perhaps worthy of mention, is that spectators who watched the film in 1922, «knew» Schønemann from the stage. In their eyes, Schønemann was not a mythical, fairytale-like figure of a long-gone past, as he may well appear to us today. By and large, 1922 audiences no doubt «heard» Schønemann's voice whenever he «uttered» something through the silent title cards onscreen, which must've greatly enhanced the film's comedic effect to them.

The film crew and stars having wrapped up the production with a vivacious party held at director Eriksen's villa,[220] they were no doubt relieved to read several positive reviews to *Kjærlighet paa Pinde* in the fall. Although one critic is said to have proclaimed that Schønemann was «funnier onstage»,[221] most reviewers offered praise when it came to his performance. As was so often the case onstage, the comedian was deemed responsible for providing the film's true *punch*:

«Without exaggeration, we can safely predict that [Schønemann] is to become an excellent film comedian,» declared a reviewer in *Morgenbladet*, following its release in early September 1922 at the former Fahlstrøm theater, where Schønemann had been employed more than a decade before and whose building, by now, screened motion-pictures fulltime.[222] The *Morgenbladet* reviewer also made it clear that the film, as the first Norwegian screen farce, should be considered an «experiment».[223]

The 4-reeler was «quite certainly the movie sensation of the month», exclaimed another critic.[224] Indeed, the brains behind the film had been wise to count on Schønemann's pulling force. *Kjærlighet paa Pinde* proved a tremendous box-office success, and was to reach Norwegian screens again throughout the silent era. (By a coincidence, the film was, for instance, to be re-screened in the town of Tvetestrand in February 1925, a mere week before Schønemann's passing.[225])

Its box-office success notwithstanding, other reviewers of the film carried a less enthusiastic tone, to put it mildly. One paper thought the story too «thin», and the gags were declared to be «old, very old» in nature. At the film's premiére in September, an unidentified short film comedy produced by «Mach-Sennett» [sic – they just couldn't get Sennett's name right in the press, it seems] was screened prior to the main feature, and according to this reviewer, the Norwegian 4-reeler did *not* compare favorably to the Sennett-film. Schønemann was *not* the one to blame, however; to the contrary, with his performance, the comedian was found to «fight bravely in his efforts to save the failure [of the film] . . .».[226]

The Norw. *Evening Post* went so far as to proclaim that, although the film had been described as a «farce» in its promotion, it would've been «more apt to describe it as a tragedy – such dismay does it cause [in the viewer] as one views it.» The reviewer conceded that the film could, perhaps, have worked as a sort of «home movie», made with the sole purpose of entertaining personal friends and family of the film crew, but for an officially released film, «one must be allowed to demand something more than nonsense such as this.» However, the same reviewer also emphasized that «Schønemann . . . with the help of a good instructor may become a truly delightful film actor. His peculiar, grotesque presence and memorable countenance could surely suit [a film] well; but it must be done with moderation. We have long ago passed the point in film history where the highpoint of comedy involves [gags such as] Schønemann losing his pants.»[227]

Schønemann 'shooting film behind Thorleif Klausen's back.' Caricature by Fredrik Christian Bødtker. (Photo: Rune Aakvik / Oslo Museum.)

A few underwhelmed reviews may not have been what concerned the film's small production crew the most, however. Casino's actor and *teatersjef*, Thorleif Klausen, was outraged that Skandinavisk Filmcentral had gone ahead with the production without his consent. Even prior to the film's release, Klausen let his rage be known in the press, maintaining that neither Schønemann, nor Conrad Arnesen had been given permission from Casino to appear in the production. With horror, Klausen referred to the many dangerous «stunts» of the film – what if something fatal had happened to Casino's great stars!

Even as the conflict evolved, Schønemann and Arnesen appear to have been kept more or less in the background. Instead, Klausen and director Eriksen were the ones to tear each other's throats in the papers. Eriksen claimed, on his part, that he «prior to the film's shooting had met with the heads [of Casino] several times to spell out the idea [of the film], and was greeted enthusiastically at the time.»[228] Klausen did not recall any such meeting with Eriksen to have taken place, on the other hand, and demanded the film to be banned altogether before its premiére, to no avail.

One wonders if all this turbulence may in part explain why Eriksen never directed another film. On the other hand, his assistant on the production, Leif Sinding, was to have a memorable career in that regard. In 1926, Sinding directed a film adaptation of Den nye lensmanden («The New Sheriff»), a play which Schønemann had performed onstage years before. (It's likely that the comedian would've been handed a significant role in the film adaptation if, again, things had turned out differently for him.) Although the director of a few more silent films, Sinding is today mostly known for the talkies Morderen uten ansikt («Murder Without a Face», 1936), De Vergeløse («The Orphans», 1939) and Tante Pose («Auntie Bag», 1940). Granted, the crime film Murder Without a Face is chiefly remembered for having been a verifiable turkey, panned by critics at the time, but his ensuing films The Orphans and Auntie Bag are considered minor classics in Norway. In The Orphans, Schønemann's friend Per Kvist had a supporting role (as did a promising young actor by the name of Harry Braude, a man of Jewish background whose life, tragically, ended a few years later in the Holocaust).[229] The shooting of Auntie Bag coinciding with Nazi Germany's occupation of Norway in the spring of 1940, Sinding's life then took a dramatic turn, as he was appointed director of Filmdirektoratet, an organization established with the purpose of assuring that all films imported to Norway were «compatible» with the occupying forces' ideology. Sinding's cooperation with the occupying forces during World War II has made him into a controversial figure in Norwegian film history, to put it mildly. He was sentenced to four years of hard labor during the legal purge in Norway after the war.[230]

Before these dramatic events, in the years following August Schønemann's passing, Leif Sinding characterized the comedian's early demise as «tragic» for the Norwegian film industry, admitting that the light farce *Kjærlighet paa Pinde* had not given Schønemann ample opportunity to capture his talent for posterity. In 1934, Sinding reflected: «What would it not have meant for Norwegian movies as a whole, had [Schønemann] lived. August Schønemann in a major screen role – it would've marked a turning point for Norwegian film production. Beloved as he was, and such an artist of his field, he would, in an instant, have popularized Norwegian movies. . . . With Schønemann still alive, the Norwegian film industry would've reached manageable terms, and its evolution would've become . . . quite different.»[231] When Sinding wrote these words in the 1930s, he could not have known that, decades later, another member of Schønemann's family was to very much contribute to the «popularization» of Norwegian movies.

Notes

212. See, for instance, *The Port Huron Times-Herald*, May 4, 1922, p. 3: «Lloyd Hamilton Talks About the Old Days in the Movies.»

213. The exact year of its production remains unknown.

214. *Aftenposten*, morning edition, August 31, 1922, p. 6.

215. Heltberg, A. (editor): *Norsk film gjennom 35 år* (Centralforlaget, 1955), p. 36.

216. *Social-Demokraten*, July 15, 1922, p. 4.

217. *Oslo Illustrerte*, No. 19, May 12, 1934.

218. *A-Magasinet,* No. 14, April 2, 1932, p. 8.

219. *Social-Demokraten*, July 15, 1922, p. 4.

220. *A-Magasinet*, No. 14, April 2, 1932, p. 8.

221. Review from newspaper *Verdens Gang* (Sept. 1922) cited in *Aftenposten*, February 25, 1970, p. 8.

222. At the time of *Kjærlighet paa Pindes* release in 1922, the movie theater in question was known as 'Admiral Palads'. In 1929, it was renamed to 'Eldorado kino', becoming the first cinema in Norway equipped for sound film screenings (*The Singing Fool* (1928) starring Al Jolson saw its Norwegian premiére there). As Eldorado, the cinema operated until its shutdown in August 2012. Currently (2022) occupying an e-sport and gaming store, it still goes by the name of Eldorado.

223. *Morgenbladet*, September 6, 1922, p. 3.

224. Nielson, p. 47.

225. *Tvetestrandsposten*, February 11, 1925, p. 3.

226. *Social-Demokraten*, September 5, 1922, p. 6.

227. *Aftenposten*, morning edition, September 5, 1922, p. 3.

228. *Social-Demokraten*, August 30, 1922, p. 3. See also *Arbeidet*, September 2, 1922, p. 6.

229. See Michelet, Marte: *Den største forbrytelsen – Ofre og gjerningsmenn i det norske Holocaust* (Gyldendal forlag, 2014). ('The Ultimate Crime – Victims and Perpetrators in the Norwegian Holocaust.')

230. *Aftenposten*, morning edition, December 2, 1950, p. 2.

231. *Oslo Illustrerte*, No. 19, May 12, 1934.

Chapter 11

Fatherhood

Not all of August Schønemann's admirers approached him with the sole hope that he may make them laugh. When asked whether Schønemann should be given the epithet of «Kristiania's greatest Don Juan», actor and 'playboy' Erling Drangsholt shrewdly responded that Schønemann was perhaps the «second greatest» (next to himself).[232] In popular magazines of the day, some even dared to joke that a few women had committed suicide for Schønemann's sake (one hopes, at least, that the claim was only said in jest). By one account, the comedian found himself overwhelmed with «dewy flowers adorned with silk ribbons and fragrant cards» each morning.[233]

Divorce between Schønemann and Kitty Normann was not yet finalized, when he made the acquaintance of another pretty dancer, also employed at Theatre Moderne (in smaller parts), 20-year old Dagmar Kristensen.[234] Dagmar still lived at home with her parents, «planing mill worker» Karl Nikolai and Marie Kristensen,[235] and four siblings, as her relationship with the comedian evolved. Her parents, apparently, were not ecstatic about their daughter's stage ambitions, but did not stand in her way as long as she could support herself with a «proper» job on the side.[236] Conscientious as she was,

Dagmar worked from morning to late at night to make ends meet – office job at daytime, dancer at Theatre Moderne in the evenings – and she maintained this schedule even after realizing that she was with a child, in spring 1922. Understandably bewildered, the young woman kept the pregnancy a secret up to last moment. There could be no doubt as to who the father was, but the possibility of engagement seems not to have been brought up, Schønemann still being legally married to (though separated from) Kitty Normann.

Late in the evening of November 13, 1922, Dagmar gave birth to a little girl in her family's apartment at Tøyen, Kristiania, two months before term and, apparently, to the great surprise of everyone present. A nurse was called for, who announced with sadness that the child would not survive the night. As had been the case upon August Schønemann's birth 31 years before, the baby seemed so frail that no one dared to hope for her survival, and a priest was immediately called to have the little one baptized before it was too late. The nurse suggested to name the baby Aud, after actress Aud Egede-Nissen (later Richter).[237]

Happily, the somber predictions of the baby's fate did not come true, as little Aud recovered in succeeding weeks. Her mother fed the baby so eagerly that the little one almost became overweight, and soon, there was no reason to worry for her health anymore.

One photograph survives of Dagmar, August Schønemann and Aud united, shot at the area of Christiania Tivoli. Aud is seated in the baby carriage. Schønemann seems to have kept at least some contact with the child and her mother within the next couple of years, although to what degree remains unclear, and Dagmar and Aud continued to live at home with Dagmar's parents for several years. August Schønemann's fatherhood seems not to have become widely known for the remainder of his life. Yours truly has found no mention of the birth in newspapers of the day. It was not until Aud became a young adult, and her own career began to hit its stride, that the kinship first received attention. The earliest press notice the author has found in which it's pointed out directly, is from fall 1945.[238]

Dagmar Kristensen and Schønemann, little Aud in the baby carriage. C. 1924. (Courtesy of Pål Pande-Rolfsen.)

Evidently, Aud had no recollection of her father as she grew up, since he passed away so early. As an adult, she was accompanied by actor and comedian Arve Opsahl to a movie theater in the city, to attend a screening of her father's film, *Kjærlighet paa Pinde*. Opsahl remarked with glee that the funny man onscreen resembled her – something others were to point out through the years, as well – but the great August Schønemann struck Aud as an alien creature, a total stranger.[239]

Surely no one could deny that the year of 1922 had produced significant events and changes in Schønemann's life, as he'd made his «debut» both onscreen as well as in fatherhood. However, by the fall, he can be said to have taken a leap *backwards* – but even then, his success remained undisputed. Schønemann had continued to perform in various oneshot matinees at Theatre Moderne, even after he'd joined Casino theater, and now, he was to return to Theatre Moderne for a new, full blown *revue*, the first to be staged there for more than a year. Benno Singer assured the press that it had «never» been his intention to abandon revues at Theatre Moderne altogether,[240] although he may also have given in to public demand. By Per Kvist's account, the public had «demanded [Schønemann's] return to revues», as they'd «longed for him to again portray several characters within a show».[241] The new show, *Kvinden du gav mig midt i planeten*[242] (hard to translate satisfyingly, but «*The Woman You Threw Right in My Head*» will have to suffice) was *not* written by Thorleif Klausen, unlike Theatre Moderne's earlier revues. As Klausen was now preoccupied at Casino, Singer had hired a «writing team» to pen the revue,[243] and the critics were not merciful, upon its premiére on October 31 – except when it came to Schønemann's performance. Especially, Schønemann enthralled audiences with a parody of his Swedish colleague and fellow revue giant, Ernst Rolf, Schønemann's impersonation of Rolf deemed an «undescribable success.» Ernst Rolf himself was present on opening night, and is said to have enjoyed Schønemann's friendly mockery as much as anyone.[244]

Ernst Ragnar Johansson (1891-1932), alias Ernst Rolf, as the public came to know him. Widely praised as the undisputed 'king of revues' in Sweden, Rolf was equally popular in Norway throughout the 1920s. (Author's collection.)

Ernst Rolf has turned up in the pages of this book more than once. As noted elsewhere, Rolf (b. Ernst Ragnar Johansson) was a native of Sweden, where he also resided throughout his life, but he enjoyed tremendous popularity also in Norway, experiencing his first big break as a performer there in the early 1910s. Although initially known as a charming and talented, but perhaps rather prototypical performer of light tunes, from 1920 onwards Rolf became primarily associated with his work in revues. Throughout the decade, he revolutionized the art of revue in Scandinavia, harvesting great inspiration from Broadway, and with this, he introduced a type of shows which came to be labeled as revues of «international fashion.» By 1922 or so, Rolf very arguably held a position as the sole stage comedian able to compete with Schønemann's popularity in Norway. He was a true *larger than life-*entertainer, of a kind hardly seen before or since in Scandinavia. Whenever an upcoming appearance of Ernst Rolf was announced in Kristiania, chaos of joy is said to have erupted among the population. In addition to an unfathomable stage charisma, Rolf possessed talent as a composer of light tunes. He often provided his own melodies in his songs, and on occasion wrote his own lyrics, as well.

Ernst Rolf, publicity portrait. (Author's collection.)

Physically, Rolf and Schønemann were each other's polar opposites: Schønemann slim and 5.2", Rolf solidly built and reaching almost two meter above ground. On the other hand, both comedians were known to inhabit a buoyant spirit and merry nature, also offstage. Tellingly, two of Rolf's best-known songs were entitled «*Bättre och bättre dag för dag*» («*Better and Better Every Day*») and «*Lägg dina sorger i en gammal säck*» («*Put All Your Sorrows in an Old, Old Sack*»). In Rolf's case, however, the success also had a tragic aspect. Beloved Norwegian comedian Leif Juster (d. 1995), who in his youth had served as Rolf's backstage dresser, recalled Rolf as «pleasant, delightful, and *mad*. Completely cuckoo.»[245] Married three times and known to suffer from mood swings, Rolf's private life was covered exstensively in the press during his lifetime, not always favorably so. A decade after Schønemann had parodied Rolf to great applause at Theatre

Moderne, on the day before Christmas Eve 1932, Rolf tried to commit suicide by drowning, in a lake nearby his own villa. He was rescued from the water in the nick of time, his two large dogs having reportedly attacked anyone who tried to save him (!), but he died of pneumonia a few days later. He was 41. At the time of his death, Rolf had recently received message that his third wife, Norwegian-born Jenny «Tutta» Rolf, had decided to move away from him, which is often cited as a possible reason behind his suicide attempt. However, by some accounts, he had suffered from a grave depression for quite a while by then, and Haakon B. Nielson suggests that Rolf may also have been exhausted by the ever-increasing pressure which came with each new revue, with Rolf being constantly expected to top previous performances – coupled with financial troubles as a result of the Great Depression.

Still others have speculated that Rolf, who was known to inhabit a «theatrical» personality, may not have genuinely intended to end his life, but (subconsciously?) expected to get rescued sooner than he did. Obviously, none of us are in a position to know what went through his mind, nearly a century later. Whatever the case, it was a profoundly tragic ending to a life which had produced a legion of joyous moments and evenings to Scandinavian audiences in the early 1900s. He left behind a one-year old son, Tom, who was to have a distinguished career as a film editor in Hollywood, editing such films as Martin Scorsese's *Taxi Driver* (1976) and Philip Kaufman's *The Right Stuff* (1983).

Fortunately, Ernst Rolf's grim ending still belonged far ahead in the future during Schønemann's lifetime, and the two 'revue kings' were to cross paths again also after the aforementioned fall of 1922, as we shall see.

The production of motion-pictures in Norway may have been on a limited scale, but it was nonetheless rising, and so was the introduction of other modern technology. Shortly before Christmas

1922, public presentations of the Magnavox sound system were organized in Kristiania, completely new technology in Norway at the time. The most memorable display of the new system took place Second Sunday of Advent at 5 o'clock P.M., at the Young's Square in central Kristiania. Rarely had such a crowd been seen in the city, other than on National Day; about 10,000 people were estimated to have shown up at the event. Certain technical challenges were unavoidable, as it turned out – at one point, the sound became too weak, and it took some time before anyone realized that the system needed new batteries – but all in all, the exhibition was declared a success. Many prominent citizens had turned up to utter a few words through the sound system, among them a young politican named Einar Gerhardsen (much later to serve as the prime minister of Norway for about two decades). Another citizen of note tried to keep his identity a secret, but to no avail – «everyone» present could immediately recognize the voice of August Schønemann through the sound system.[246]

Furthermore, at least 30 gramophone records featuring Schønemann were made around this time, preserving some of his best-known songs for posterity. Sadly, as far as the author knows, only a few are known to exist today. Of course, even the ones that do survive conserve only a limited facet of Schønemann's repertoire and appeal. It's left to our imagination to ponder on the magic he must've added to the tunes, as he entered the stage to perform them *live*. Also, the sound quality is not very good, as is to be expected. Even so, these recordings offer the most valuable resource to anyone eager to «experience» August Schønemann in our times, as they probably tell us more about him as an artist than the film *Kjærlighet paa Pinde*. There is, for instance, the little song of *Paa bøljan den blaa* (*«On the Blue, Blue Waves»*), written by Ørnulf Dehn,[247] about a sailor who is betrayed by his sweetheart Amanda, a very simple tune which Schønemann manages to make his own through his energetic delivery. Each time he reaches the end of a verse, he «stretches» his vocal cords like a rubber band, adding a quick adlib (translated): «...*I stood there, like a shipwre-ecked maaaa-aaaaan* – that was a long one, huh! – *aaaaa-nnnnn!!!* – *on lov-ve's ocean-nnnn!!!*» Such fantastic enthusiasm, even when heard on a century-old record of subpar quality. Again, we may just imagine the impact he left on the rows of fans at Theatre Moderne while performing this and other tunes, in the early 1920s.

Notes

232. Magazine clipping found among Aug. Schønemann's personal papers, although not stored in the scrapbook. 1919.

233. Ibid.

234. Dagmar was born November 3, 1901; see 1910 Census for Kristiania, Census district 123, Urban residence 0021 Heimdalsgt. 36.

235. Ibid. The father, Karl N., b. 1875; the mother, Marie, b. 1876. See also Confirmations: 1916-05-14, Church book from Tøyen parish 1907-1916 (0301M23).

236. Gulbrandsen, Lars O., p. 16.

237. Ibid., p. 11.

238. *Dagbladet*, September 21, 1945, p. 3.

239. Gulbrandsen, Lars O., p. 23.

240. *Dagbladet*, December 15, 1921, p. 7.

241. *Arbeiderbladet*, July 29, 1939, p. 8. Essay by Per Kvist.

242. *Dagbladet*, October 31, 1922, p. 4.

243. *Arbeider-Politikken*, November 1, 1922, p. 1.

244. Ibid.

245. TV interview with Leif Juster. NRK, November 13, 1976.

246. *Social-Demokraten*, December 4, 1922, p. 6.

247. Norwegian lyrics printed in *August Schønemanns komiske viser* (Otto Stenersens Boktrykkeri, Kristiania, 192?).

Chapter 12

Comedy King Meets Ex-Emperor

New Year of 1923. More than four years had passed since the end of the Great War, Italy's victory during the Battle of Vittorio Veneto, in late fall 1918, having settled the final outcome. With the double-monarchy of Austria-Hungary dissolved, Germany was forced to admit defeat. A binding peace treaty was eventually set up.

Regardless, as is well known, the War's aftermath was to affect Europe for years afterward. Between 14 and 17 million people are estimated to have lost their lives as a result of the war, and even more were physically or mentally injured, often for life. In Norway, the number of fatalities was not on a scale comparable to France, Germany and many other European countries, but also here, a high number of people had lost their lives at sea as a direct consequence of the war, as mentioned previously. Although by 1923, the population at large may have managed to achieve some distance to the war, its horrors remained in fresh memory to plenty of people.

For many, the ability to *laugh* at the madness, at least every now and then, could not be underestimated for its therapeutic powers. A few gifted comedians managed to make great humor with the War in mind, in a way that did not strike audiences as offensive. Charlie Chaplin's three-reel film, *Shoulder Arms* (1918), stands as particularly famous, with Charlie's brother Sydney portraying Emperor Wilhelm II of Germany.

Emperor Wilhelm II's «legacy» is said to have undergone a significant change through the years. In later decades, he has been typically portrayed as a politically naïve man, perhaps out of sync with the changing world around him at the time of the War's outbreak. Apparently, this view began to take form around the time of Hitler's rise to power in the early 1930s;[248] compared to Hitler, Emperor Wilhelm II simply appeared less terrifying (or evil) to people. On the other hand, in the years immediately following The Great War, it was relatively common to see Wilhelm depicted as more of a traditional «villain» in popular culture.

Without doubt, historians will have various opinions on which depiction of Wilhelm II that comes closest to the truth. In any case, we can safely assume it to have been no small feat for any actor to portray the resigned Emperor in the aftermath of The Great War, considering how he was often perceived at the time – but in January 1923, audiences were to spot August Schønemann doing precisely that role. Equipped with the «Emperor's» wide moustache, its ends turned upward, and sporting a reasonably convincing «German» military outfit, Schønemann majestically entered the revue of *Storting og Smaating* at Theatre Moderne (the title offers a pun difficult to translate, but a literal translation would be «*Parliament and Little Things*»). He is said to have done a priceless figure. A critic of the Norw. *Evening Post*, although not uncritical of the revue as a whole, singled out Schønemann's impersonation of *der Kaiser* as the show's «saving force».[249] In the role, Schønemann performed the five-verse song, «*Ekskeiser Wilhelms vise*» («*Former Emperor Wilhelm's Tune*») – it's probably not advisable to attempt a translation of the lyrics here, made up as they are of an anarchic blend of Norwegian slang and German, but one line goes:

«Es ist fatalt mit Ruhr ja und mit Essen,
hvad skal de der? Gott strafe Poincare!»[250]

(The last line refers, of course, to Raymond Poincaré, who'd served as president of France during World War I.)

Schønemann as 'Emperor Wilhelm II', in the revue Storting og Smaating *at Theatre Moderne. Newspaper photo,* Aftenposten *morning edition, January 20, 1923.*

Storting og Smaating ran for almost three months,[251] and the comedian's take on the Emperor was to remain one of his most well-remembered performances in retrospect. Following the final act one evening, Schønemann was handed flower bouquets onstage while audiences screamed with delight, after which the revue's author entered the stage to read a poem in honor of the comedian, and put a «golden crown» on his head.[252]

By now, August Schønemann was only to be regarded as a «guest star» in the revues at Theatre Moderne, however. Shortly after the final performance of *Storting og Smaating*, he returned to Casino, scheduled to appear in a play which had generated a huge amount of publicity on beforehand: Erik Bøgh's stage adaptation of Jules Verne's immortal novel, *Around the World in 80 Days*, with Schønemann portraying servant Passepartout. Although Casino had primarily relied on staging operettas since the theater's grand opening two years prior, they now sought to broaden their repertoire a bit.

Schønemann was nothing less than ecstatic about the role of Passepartout, as it provided him with an abundance of opportunities to showcase his improvisational skills – one time unintentionally so, as Thorleif Klausen vividly recalled nearly a decade later: as most readers are probably aware, much of *Around the World in 80 Days* takes place on a long train ride, and Casino theater spared no expenses. The theater had a large, human-sized «toy locomotive» built for the scene, which for the most part worked flawlessly – but at one performance, the «locomotive» suddenly rolled off the rails by mistake, trundling offstage. Reportedly, Schønemann gave the derailed vehicle a quick glance, and quipped: «Now I get what the term *rolling stock* means.» The locomotive having been fixed in a hurry and put back onstage again as though nothing had happened, Schønemann could not resist another adlib: «Look at that,» he said, «as good as new. It sure ain't easy to knock down the ol' West Line!» (The «West Railway Line», or *Vestbanen* of Norway, had experienced a scandal that spring.)

«Loud cheers» were heard, recalled Klausen.[253]

Selmer som **Phileas Fogg**, **Schønemann som Passepartout** og **Klausen som detektiv Fix**.

Caricature of Jens Selmer (Phileas Fogg), Schønemann (Passepartout) and Thorleif Klausen (Detective Fix) in Around the World in 80 Days *at Casino theater. Aftenposten, April 28, 1923.*

The Norw. *Evening Post* had, for a change, almost only superlatives to offer this time around. «[The play] carries a red line [in terms of story] which a modern revue almost never does,» the critic opined. «The older [spectators] may feel to have dug up an old, familiar novel of their youth . . . while for the young ones, 'Around the World' is a true adventure. Statistics of Kristiania reveal that the city houses a phenomenal number of families with young boys, so Mr. [Thorleif] Klausen may safely give orders to polish the glass of the [theater's] red light. It shall burn often.»

Similar stage adaptations of *Around the World in 80 Days* had reached theaters in Denmark and Sweden prior to Norway, and the critic of the Norw. *Evening Post* could not resist to declare, having seen it performed in all three countries, that no Danish or Swedish actor could match August Schønemann's Passepartout, in his (arguably biased) opinion.[254]

✳✳✳

Swedish Ernst Rolf was in full vigour this year. As noted above, citizens of Kristiania were overwhelmed with joy whenever Rolf was scheduled to appear in the city, and this particular summer, his popularity would reach nigh on epic heights. On Sunday, July 1 at eight o'clock P.M., «Rolf's Revue of 1923», a 3-act show by the name of *Fra Karl Johan til Lykkeland*, had its premiére at Casino[255] (its title referring to the main street of Kristiania known as «Karl Johan», a plausible translation would perhaps be *«From Karl Johan to Paradise»*). A more extravagant revue had not been seen in the country's history, magnificent costumes and stage sets having been imported from abroad.[256] Throughout the show, Rolf performed, among other things, six songs, all of which became smash hits of the day. In the final act, Rolf entered the stage in white smoking, and threw himself into a huge aquarium onstage (reportedly containing 150.000 litres of water), fully dressed!

From 'Ernst Rolf's Revue of 1923', Fra Karl Johan til Lykkeland *at Casino, 1923. Schønemann sitting. (Nasjonalbiblioteket / The National Norwegian Library.)*

As one may well expect, Ernst Rolf was promoted as the main star of this costly revue, but Casino could not let an appearance by Schønemann go to waste for that reason. The thought of intertwining the two comedy giants in the same show was irresistible, and in the role of a «Lion trainer», Schønemann can be said to have accorded the revue its extra spicing. Alongside his portrayal of the Neutrality guard from *Futt*, the «Lion trainer» sketch probably stands as Schønemann's most legendary stage accomplishment today. Loosely based on a British comedy script, the sketch had been penned by a well-known Norwegian bookseller named Jacob Dybwad.

Dance number from Fra Karl Johan til Lykkeland, *1923. (Nasjonalbiblioteket / The Norwegian National Library.)*

One would, perhaps, be tempted to think that Schønemann was here handed a rather majestetic role – a lion trainer! – but, as it turned out, his role in the sketch was that of a hapless, browbeaten husband, who is thrown into the job of lion training by his wife Augusta (alternately played by Signe Heide-Steen and Ebba Toje), very much against his will.

As luck will have it, the script of the «Lion trainer» sketch survives. Reading it today, as mere text, it's perhaps not entirely obvious why it became such a sensation. As Schønemann's friend Per Kvist recalled, «the words [in the sketch] were not as vital as the facial expressions [of the performers]». As «Alfred's» stern wife threatened his unlucky husband to apply for a job as a lion trainer, «Schønemann's gestures captured any perceivable shade of fear and horror, so that [the public] felt with him even as we laughed ourselves silly.»[257] Be that as it may: are we, perhaps, capable of imagining Schønemann and Signe Heide-Steen – or Ebba Toje – onstage before us in our minds, as we now read through the script, which supplied the public with such fond memories at the time? (Once again, certain typical «Norwegian phrases» are hard to translate satisfyingly, but I have done my best here.)

Schønemann as 'Alfred,' the henpecked husband who gets thrown into the profession of lion training, very much against his will. 1923. (Nasjonalbiblioteket / The Norwegian National Library.)

(The stage depicts the entrance of «Kempinski Circus.» A large sign reads: 'Lion trainer wanted.' A shoddily clothed woman [«Augusta»] enters, accompanied by her unemployed husband [Schønemann, «Alfred»].)

Augusta: Where're you going, Alfred dear?

Alfred: I thought I might's well stand here and watch those who can afford to go inside [and watch the circus].

Augusta: I think you better not, that's not proper, Alfred. – Where did you put the quarter I gave you yesterday?

Alfred: I bought myself a cigar.

Augusta: Such an idiot. Don't talk to me.

Alfred: I thought you talked in your sleep, Augusta.

Augusta: In my *sleep*? [Speaks to herself.] Oh, what a character, and he thinks *he'll* get a job.

Alfred: Speak not of work, Augusta. I get weary by the mere thought of it.

Augusta: I wish you sat in the lion's cage!

Alfred: Speak not of lions, either, Augusta!

Augusta: But what am I to *do* with you, fellow?

Alfred: I enjoy the company of canary birds more than I do lions.

Augusta (stern): Alfred, *when* will you get a job?

Alfred: Dear woman, you need not to worry about that. So long as one's got patience, one's wishes will come true in the end, and so, too, will work.

Augusta: Well, my patience is all spent, so I tell you, the next job proposal you encounter, you *will* accept, no matter what!

Alfred: No matter what?

Augusta: Oh yes, and I am about to get you one, at once. Here it is!

Alfred: Where?

(Augusta points at the 'Lion trainer wanted' sign. Alfred paralyzed with shock.)

Augusta: As though sent from heaven.

Alfred: Rather from the opposite direction, I'd say.

Augusta: Oh, if only you got that job...

Alfred: Then you'd get the life insurance, I bet.

Augusta: Just think, such an excellent occupation!

Alfred: For the *lion*, perhaps!

Augusta: Don't be silly, Alfred, you were *born* to perform lion dressage.

Alfred: What's that? I thought you said I's born to be a lion's dessert!

(Circus manager enters.)

Manager: Enter, ladies and gentlemen, please enter!

Alfred: I've still *not* got that job, thank goodness.

Augusta: Just you wait, you will get it. I'll talk to the manager.

Alfred: He ain't no manager, he feeds wild animals.

Augusta: That amounts to the same. How do you do, Mr. Manager.

Manager: How do you do, Madam.

Augusta: Are you the head of the circus?

Manager: That is correct, Madam. Alexander Gambetta Kempinski.

Augusta: Oh, and you look like it, too. Anyway, I understand you're seeking a lion trainer. *You* need a lion trainer; well, *here* he stands.

Alfred: I feel weird. *(Lion roars in the distance.)* What was that?

Manager: That's the lion. Are you fond of lions?

Augusta: This is my husband, Mr. Manager, he is all *wild* about lions – are you not, Alfred?

Alfred: Oh yes indeed, yes indeed. Preferably tiny wooden lions on wheels. Or like the *Storting* lions [*note:* the front entrance of the Norwegian *Storting*, Parliament, is adorned with two large «lions» made of granite].

Augusta: He simply cannot *live* without lions, he's been   *brought up* among lions.

Alfred: Boast not so much on my behalf, woman!

Augusta: He'll speak of *nothing* but lions, lions in the mornings, afternoons, and at night. I can't make him think of anything else. Talk to the manager, now, Alfred, and I am sure you'll get the job. I'll wait outside. *(Exits.)*

Manager: Have you ever stuck your head into a lion's mouth?

Alfred: What's that? Oh well, I guess it's possible, but I certainly cannot recall it.

Manager: You're just the man we need. *(Shakes Alfred's hand.)*

(Lion's roar heard again. Two men carry a dead man on a stretcher across the stage.)

Alfred: Who's that?

Manager: That's the guy you're replacing. You're not nervous, are you?

Alfred (shaking): No, no, I was just up dancing all night...

Manager: We're willing to give you a trial period of a week, would that satisfy you?

Alfred: It should satisfy the lions, I bet.

Manager: You may practice on the baby lion, as warmup.

(Lion roars again.)

Alfred: Was that the baby lion?

Manager: It's just a baby yet, fed on fresh milk.

Alfred: So was I once, but I mostly eat meat these days...

Manager (hands Alfred a whip): Should it ever bother you, you just strike it with this one, and say, 'Couche!'

Alfred: Strike the lion – do you think it'll obey me then?

Manager: One can never trust a lion, they're sneaky.

Alfred: Could we not ask it firsthand, whether it's dangerous? *(Alfred walks into the lion's cage, trembling with fear. Lion roars. Augusta reappears.)*

Augusta: Alfred, Alfred, where are you, where are you!

Manager: He just entered the lion's cage.

Augusta: Good Lord! They'll tear him to pieces, help!

Manager: Be calm, Madam. It'll soon be over.

Augusta: Alfred, my husband, my poor husband!

(Roars and noises are heard. Silence. Two men carry a stretcher across the stage again. On the stretcher is a dead lion. Alfred reappears. Walks to the 'Lion trainer wanted' sign and tears off the word 'trainer', so the sign reads: 'Lion wanted.')258

Impossible to reproduce on these pages, as noted above, are the distorted facial expressions of poor «Alfred» throughout the scene. Fortunately, a number of photographs of Schønemann dressed as «Alfred» survive.

The public reception to *Fra Karl Johan til Lykkeland* can hardly be exaggerated. With this show, Casino had produced one of Norway's grandest theatrical events of the decade. Performed until late October 1923, the auditorium remained crowded throughout its four-month run. By now, one would perhaps think that not even August Schønemann could reach any higher, but indeed he could – although sadly, he lived on borrowed time, as it turned out.

Notes

248. Carlin, Dan (podcast): *Hardcore History 50 – Blueprint for Armageddon I.* October 29, 2013.

249. *Aftenposten*, morning edition, January 20, 1923, p. 7.

250. «Lyktemanden»: *Ta hornbriller paa og andre viser* (O. Gjeruldsens forlag), 1924, p. 38.

251. *Arbeiderbladet*, April 14, 1923, p. 4.

252. *Aftenposten*, morning edition, March 5, 1923, p. 5.

253. *Humør 1932* (Klausen, Thorleif), pp. 135-136.

254. *Aftenposten*, morning edition, April 28, 1923, p. 2.

255. *Aftenposten*, June 30, 1923, p. 8.

256. Nielson, p. 50.

257. *Arbeiderbladet*, July 29, 1939, p. 10. Essay by Per Kvist.

258. *Humør 1932*, pp. 139-148. Translated from Norwegian by yours truly; any errors are purely my own.

Chapter 13

Without A Thread

It had not been Casino's intention to let the revue *Fra Karl Johan til Lykkeland* enjoy such a long run, but the influx of spectators remained constant even as the fall approached, so much so that no one thought it defensible to end it. Ticket sales fared «better and better» each day, cheered *teatersjef* Klausen in an interview in the late summer.[259]

Finally, however, Casino's grand success had to be laid to rest, to make room for their great show of fall 1923, the 3-act operetta *Prince Don Juan*, with music by Victor Corzilius. A comic intrigue starring Ragnar Wingar as a destitute prince, and co-starring Thorleif Klausen, Schønemann here played a young orphan.[260] Although partly intended as a sort of compromise for the theater to get itself together after the busy summer, also with this operetta Casino could be counted on to provide audiences with «decent melodies, vibrant colors, and fantastic costumes.»[261] The play was deemed to have mostly run its course after only a month, however, after which it was performed for «afternoon performances» at reduced prices until mid-December.

His busy schedule notwithstanding, Schønemann appears to have found time for a week's «vacation» in Copenhagen in late November, after which he spent a few days in Stockholm.[262] One may well understand his need for a change of scenery, but he was back in Kristiania again by December 8, when he appeared at the concert hall of Gamle Logen, doing a benefit performance to raise money to «unemployed trade officials in Kristiania and destitute German colleagues»[263] (the unemployment rate and economic situation in Germany being absolutely precarious at this point).

Although a fair success by most standards, the aforementioned operetta *Prince Don Juan* did not become one of Casino's truly greatest triumphs. On the other hand, the theater was to stir considerable anticipation in the press when it was announced that Gilbert & Sullivan's famous operetta, *The Mikado*, was next out on their program, its premiére held on December 26, 1923 after some weeks' delay. As with Ernst Rolf's revue the previous summer, audiences could certainly count on getting their money's worth; nearly all costumes, as well as most of the sets, had been ordered directly from Berlin, with none other than German-Austrian Max Reinhardt serving as director.[264] *The Mikado*, of course, had swept across Europe in numerous renditions, ever since its original run in London in 1885. Set in a fictionalized «Japanese» environment, Gilbert & Sullivan are thought to have used «Japan» in their play merely as a cover, to satirize aspects of British society and get away with it. In the play, the son of the «Japanese Mikado», Nanki-Poo, runs away from home to avoid marriage to an older woman. Disguised as a vagabond musician, Nanki-Poo encounters the girl Yum-Yum while on his way, who is maid to an impoverished hangman and tailor named Ko-Ko. Intricacies evolve as the runaway, of course, falls in love with Yum-Yum.

From Casino theater's staging of Gilbert & Sullivan's The Mikado, *early 1924. Schønemann as executioner Ko-Ko to the right. Newspaper photo. Dagsposten, January 15, 1924. (Author's collection.)*

Not surprisingly, Conrad Arnesen was handed the role of handsome Nanki-Poo, while Thorleif Klausen appeared as the «Mikado» himself. The «gloomy stage character»[265] of hangman-tailor Ko-Ko, meanwhile, stood at Schønemann's disposal. Not exactly intended as a likable character, as Ko-Ko Schønemann was nonetheless expected to perform the sentimental song *Blåkjelken* («*The Blue Sledge*»). Schønemann and Reinhardt agreed that the ballad should be performed without so much as a trace of comedy, despite Ko-Ko's clownish appearance. While Schønemann was widely praised as the funniest man of Norway for nearly a decade by this point, the sentiment of this song would give the comedian an opportunity to broaden his repertoire, but the question remained: *would the public «get it»?*

Seldom had Schønemann felt such nerves prior to a performance, when the time was ripe for his rendition of *Blåkjelken* at the *Mikado* première, a mere day after Christmas morning. Dressed as Ko-Ko in magnificent «Japanese» silk, and contemplating the crowd before him with melancholy eyes, Schønemann performed his heartbreaker of a song with complete sincerity – and was met with immense jubilation. Certainly, no one had expected *this*! Schønemann himself is said to have been most overwhelmed of all, however. Once the performance was done with, he reportedly hurried backstage and burst out crying.[266]

«Schønemann is soon to become a first-rate actor of operettas – or, he is one already,» avowed the Norw. *Evening Post*.[267]

Behind the scenes, the comedian's brief marriage to Kitty Normann was now formally dissolved, two years having passed since the couple went separate ways, and a year after Dagmar Kristensen had given birth to little Aud.

The Mikado ran for a total of 45 performances, until February 1924.[268] Another farce operetta then found its way onto Casino's stage, this time set in a «bathing hotel»: Leo Kastner and Hans H. Zerlett's 3-act *Grand Hotel Amor*,[269] again starring Klausen, Arnesen and Schønemann, as well as up-and-coming, 21-year old Sigrun Svenningsen, an actress later to marry Schønemann's friend Per Kvist. Although one reviewer deemed Schønemann's «yankee-inspired» character in *Grand Hotel Amor* as «unsuited» for his talents, the comedian was found «to do his best» with the material given him.[270]

Schønemann's days at Casino were now numbered, however. *Grand Hotel Amor* was immediately followed by another Jules Verne-adaptation, *Kaptein Grants barn* («*In Search of the Castaways*»), premiéring on April 26.[271] Relying heavily on Verne's novel, the play's plot occurred partly on a «Pacific island», as well as in a fictionalized South America and Australia, with Thorleif Klausen starring as Captain Grant, Conrad Arnesen doing Lord Eduard Glenarvan, while the role of the absent-minded professor, Paganel, was handed to Schønemann. Klausen served as director this time around. While the house was as crowded as one could wish for upon the première, critics were more mixed than what had been the case with *Around the World...*: «It was disheartening to witness some of the theater's truly great forces go to waste in this childish and banal tableau», snorted *Nationen*. «The only one among them who came off well was Schønemann, who in characteristic fashion delivered his comic tricks to an immensely grateful public.»[272]

Schønemann as the absent-minded professor Paganel, in Casino's staging of Jules Verne's In Search of the Castaways, *spring 1924. (Photo: Thorleif Wardenær / Oslo Museum.) (This work is licensed under the Creative Commons Attribution-ShareAlike 4.0 International License. To view a copy of this license, visit http://creativecommons.org/licenses/ by-sa/4.0/ or send a letter to Creative Commons, PO Box 1866, Mountain View, CA 94042, USA.)*

Nonetheless, *In Search of the Castaways* was to enjoy a respectable run, with performances held until June 1924.[273] Thereafter, as summer again made its entrance, Schønemann *sort of* announced his return to Theatre Moderne for another revue – that is, the revue would technically be staged at Casino, as Benno Singer decided to let Theatre Moderne use Casino for its summer performances that year (likely because Casino could room more spectators). Its première having already occurred on May 29, Schønemann thus joined the revue of *Cirkus Christiania*[274] at Theatre Moderne/Casino from June 12. According to one reviewer, he made a particular impression in the role of an «inventor Sebædæus Rukke»,[275] but others were less ecstatic: «It's an abuse of talent to let Schønemann go to waste for an entire summer in this revue», a critic remarked, although despite a number of «weak» songs and jokes, the public seemed to have «enjoyed the evening», and Schønemann in particular.[276]

Schønemann's semi-comeback at «Theatre Moderne» was to be brief, however. Heads of other theater venues had their eyes on him, among them Victor Bernau, leader of Chat Noir. Established in 1912, Chat Noir had evolved into a popular theater of light entertainment under Bernau's leadership. Later iconic figures such as Jens Book-Jensen – nicknamed the «Bing Crosby of Norway» in the 1930s – still belonged to the future at Chat Noir, but once there, Schønemann was to reach an even broader audience than before, as he «skyrocketed right up to the finest of theater spheres.»[277] The details as to how Bernau «acquired» Schønemann for Chat Noir, are not fully clear. According to one news item from January 1924, «rumors» circulated that Benno Singer had made an agreement with Bernau. Both Casino *and* Chat Noir were to have almost their entire staff discharged and replaced, it was claimed, while Bernau was to hire Schønemann in the hope of transforming Chat Noir into a prominent «revue theater» (at which he was to succeed, as it turned out).[278] Schønemann's exact salary when signing his contract at Chat Noir is disputed; Nielson states it to have been nearly 20,000 Crowns per season,[279] while press notices of the time claimed it amounted to 24,000 Crowns, «reportedly the highest salary of any actor in the nation» at the time, or about $61,000 today.[280] (It bears mentioning that Norway was still very much feeling the effects of the economic crisis from the early 1920s. The economic growth which the States and some European countries experienced during the decade, did not truly enter Norwegian reality until about 1928.) Although a giant among Norwegian entertainers by now, even Schønemann may have trembled for a bit as he signed his contract at Chat Noir. Whether 20,000 or 24,000 Crowns, in a Norwegian context, Schønemann's new salary was enormous for an actor at the time.

Almost unbearable excitement echoed in the lobby of Chat Noir as their grand revue of the fall, *Uten en tråd* («*Without a Thread*») was ripe for première on September 1, 1924. «Never has Chat Noir had better personnel at their disposal,» the verdict read,[281] which may indeed have been true. Schønemann was, among others, accompanied by Bernau, his friend Per Kvist, and Swedish soprano Märta Reiners, names which may not ring any bells to most readers today, but they certainly evoked instant recognition to stagestruck Norwegians of the 1920s.

As one may well guess, based on its title, *Without a Thread* did not carry any «plot» to speak of, unlike most of the productions in which Schønemann had appeared at Casino. Moreover, the revue at Chat Noir was even more episodic in nature than most of Theatre Moderne's revues, displaying an almost frantic tempo throughout (an emerging 'comedy style' which was to gain increasing popularity in Norwegian revues in the coming years, but which may have struck certain segments of the public as rather bizarre at the time). The lack of «story» didn't matter much, thought one critic; after all, in a revue without a plot, audiences were served «exactly the confetti that is the proper stimulus to any individual of our busy times.» Schønemann appeared in numerous roles and costumes throughout the show, including that of a «barber», and his «facial expressions and comic devices» were found to be «incomparable.»[282] A «Tyrol parody» turned out to become one of the biggest crowdpleasers of the revue, featuring Schønemann as the «dream prince Pieter», while actresses Ingeborg «Botten» Soot and Lalla Carlsen played «yodeling girls»[283] (Carlsen, in particular, was soon to attain considerable fame as a performer in her own right).

The "Tyrol parody" in the revue Uten en traad *('Without a Thread') at Chat Noir, fall 1924. Schønemann alongside Lalla Carlsen (left) and Ingeborg 'Botten' Soot (right). (Photo: Unknown / Oslo Museum.) (This work is licensed under the Creative Commons Attribution-ShareAlike 4.0 International License. To view a copy of this license, visit http://creativecommons.org/licenses/by-sa/4.0/ or send a letter to Creative Commons, PO Box 1866, Mountain View, CA 94042, USA.)*

It warrants a mention that the première of *Without a Thread* coincided with a grand, 25th anniversary performance held at the Norwegian National Theater nearby the very same evening, starring leading actor Hauk Aabel among others.[284] Whether this was a question of bad timing for both parties (unlikely), or a deliberate stunt by Chat Noir to prove that they could indeed rival the National Theater if they so desired (more likely), Chat Noir needed not to worry: instant success was a fact. As had been the case with so many of the «plotless» revues at Theatre Moderne, *Without a Thread* was interspersed with new sketches and characters throughout its run. Not only did the actors themselves likely welcome this; it also assured constant audience attendance, as spectators with a few dimes to spare may have been tempted to attend the show more than once.

Most immortal of all the characters which Schønemann portrayed during the revue's sixteen-week run – and what turned out to be the culmination of a spectacular career – was that of «Hamlet», or rather, a parody on dramatic actor Ingolf Schanche's interpretation of the famous Danish Prince. Employed at the National Theater in Kristiania since a number of years back, Schanche knew Hamlet inside out, having even received an offer to do the role in Paris.[285] One may wonder how *he* responded to Schønemann's caricature! The aforementioned Lalla Carlsen stood by Schønemann's side in the role of Ophelia.[286] As one studies still photographs of Schønemann as «Hamlet», it seems far from evident that his performance was intended as *parody*. In one photograph in particular, the one thing that may reveal it to be «merely» a humorous interpretation is the skull resting in his hand, which looks a bit comic and «rubberlike». Otherwise, he comes off as astoundingly graceful while posing as the haunted prince.

Without a Thread ran without break until New Year of 1925, as one of the most enduring of all the theater productions which Schønemann had been involved in. None of the spectators who cheered Schønemann as he seized the stage as «Hamlet» – indeed, no one beyond his inner circle – had the slightest idea that he suffered horrific pains every night.

Lalla Carlsen as Ophelia, Schønemann as Hamlet. From their "Hamlet" parody in the revue Uten en traad *at Chat Noir, fall 1924. (Photo: Fotocentralen a.s. / Oslo Museum) (This work is licensed under the Creative Commons Attribution-ShareAlike 4.0 International License. To view a copy of this license, visit http://creativecommons.org/licenses/ by-sa/4.0/ or send a letter to Creative Commons, PO Box 1866, Mountain View, CA 94042, USA.)*

Notes

259. *Aftenposten,* morning edition, August 10, 1923, p. 7.

260. *Nationen,* October 31, 1923, p. 3.

261. *Dagbladet,* October 29, 1923, p. 4.

262. *Morgenbladet*, December 1, 1923, p. 3.

263. *Arbeiderbladet*, December 6, 1923, p. 9. See also *Social-Demokraten*, December 8, 1923, p. 5.

264. *Aftenposten*, morning edition, August 10, 1923, p. 7.

265. Nielson, pp. 43-44.

266. Ibid., pp. 43-46.

267. *Aftenposten*, morning edition, December 27, 1923, p. 6.

268. *Arbeiderbladet*, February 8, 1924, p. 4.

269. *Aftenposten*, morning edition, February 11, 1924, p. 2.

270. *Nationen*, February 11, 1924, p. 2.

271. *Arbeiderbladet*, April 25, 1924, p. 7. Haakon B. Nielson states the premiére of *In Search of the Castaways* to have taken place on April 17 (Nielson, p. 42), but newspaper notices suggest that April 25 is correct. It's possible that a preview performance was held on the date which Nielson cites.

272. *Nationen*, April 28, 1924, p. 3.

273. The cast went on tour around Norway with the play later in 1924, but then without Schønemann's participation.

274. *Dagbladet*, June 7, 1924, p. 4.

275. *Morgenbladet*, June 27, 1924, p. 5.

276. *Christiania Nyheds- og Advertissements-Blad («Morgenposten»)*, July 10, 1924, p. 3.

277. *Dagbladet*, September 2, 1924, p. 2.

278. *Christiania Nyheds- og Advertissementsblad*, January 18, 1924, p. 4.

279. Nielson, p. 52.

280. *Fredrikshalds Avis*, February 2, 1924, p. 2. See also *Morgenavisen*, February 7, 1924, p. 4, and numerous other Norwegian papers of the same month.

281. *Arbeiderbladet*, August 28, 1924, p. 6.

282. *Arbeiderbladet*, September 2, 1924, p. 2. See also Nielson, p. 52.

283. *Nå* magazine, #3/1959, pp. 20-21.

284. *Dagbladet*, September 2, 1924, p. 1.

285. *1ste Mai*, May 26, 1924, p. 3.

286. Nielson, pp. 52-54. See also *Dagbladet*, October 18, 1924, p. 2.

Chapter 14

Idol of the Gallery

Aspiring film director Leif Sinding still had hopes of luring Schønemann back in front of the camera, to star in a «real» silver screen production. Nearly two years had passed since the making of *Kjærlighet paa Pinde* when Sinding, sometime in 1924 – probably a bit prior to Schønemann's first appearance at Chat Noir – approached the comedian with such an errand in mind. Chatting together backstage, we may see before us Schønemann as he wiped away makeup from his face, while Sinding outlined his proposal: it was the popular Norwegian «folk comedy», *Til sæters* («*To the Mountain Pastures*») that was to be adapted to the screen, a play which Schønemann knew from his modest beginnings as an actor, way back in 1907. Not only would Schønemann's appearance assure the film its success at the box-office; moreover, he would be given the chance to shine in a «real» role onscreen! Old acquaintances of his were to appear alongside him, among them Ellen Sinding and Signe Heide-Steen.

Leif Sinding was not greeted in the manner he expected, however. According to Sinding, Schønemann stared at him for a while, with a look of «infinite despair and hopelessness.» Finally, the comedian bluntly uttered that it was impossible, he could not get himself involved in another film production, *not at all*. At first, Sinding refused to take no for an answer, but Schønemann remained adamant, until he, by Sinding's account, burst out: «Don't you think I *want to*? Oh, yes, for sure, I do. I believe in the movies . . . But I cannot, absolutely not. I am finished. I can't take it anymore. . . .»

Sinding was shocked by this behavior, coming as it did from a man known to «always joke his way out of any gloom.» Realizing that Schønemann was not to be convinced, Sinding left the room without results.[287] (The film was released in the late fall of 1924, sans Schønemann, with Harry Ivarson serving as director.)

Of course, this summary of the conversation between Schønemann and Leif Sinding that night reflects only Sinding's account, and we do not know whether he may have embellished it in retrospect. Regardless, there can be no doubt that Schønemann's seemingly indestructible spirit had begun to wear down at this point. His later appearances at Casino had been marked with exhaustion, dizziness and chest pains, and his condition only worsened during the fall at Chat Noir. It seems that, many a night, he'd had to drag himself backstage in pain after a performance of *Without a Thread*.[288] His co-star Lalla Carlsen, who'd known Schønemann for about a decade and had fond memories of his many pranks and jokes, recalled that she and actress Botten Soot were obliged to literally carry him offstage at times, which they solved by seating him in a «golden chair» included in their «Tyrol parody» sketch, so as not to raise suspicion among audiences that anything was wrong (Schønemann «wasn't very heavy», Carlsen remembered).[289] As the season continued, Schønemann felt so exhausted after each night's performance that he could not even be persuaded to remain for applause as the curtains went down, instead standing against the wall backstage while breathing heavily in pain.

Nevertheless, for months Schønemann refused to let any of the excruciating symptoms get in the way of his performances, perhaps declaring it a matter of professional honor to not leave an audience disappointed. Never should anyone *pity* the funniest man of Norway!

In early December 1924, Schønemann went on a brief tour, to perform his *second* play alongside Chat Noir's ensemble, the 3-act farce *Vor lille frue* («*Little Miss Bluebeard*»), written by famed Broadway playwright Avery Hopwood.[290] Chat Noir reserved the Kristiania première of the play for the holidays, December 26.[291] The public still oblivious to the comedian's critical condition, one critic wrote that there «was not a dead moment throughout the performance» to be found, and «the performers [Kirsten] Monrad Aas, [Victor] Bernau and Schønemann certainly managed to keep the good mood going.»[292] (As a sidenote: on January 1, Kristiania was given back its old name of Oslo, after 300 years.)

With Schønemann now being in such frail health, however, his participation in the play could go on for only so long. *Little Miss Bluebeard* had been running for about a month when the Norw. *Evening Post* reported, on January 13, 1925, that Schønemann was on «sick leave» from Chat Noir, his role «temporarily» handed to actor Josef Sjøgren[293] (who'd played opposite Schønemann as «Charlie Chaplin» at Theatre Moderne several years before). No explanation was given, and the public probably saw no cause for alarm. A month later, one reviewer casually remarked that he «missed» Schønemann's presence in the revue,[294] but that was that.

Despite all his pains, Schønemann had, reportedly, refused to go for a checkup. He is said to have feared doctors,[295] like many of his generation. As much as one may understand this from a 1920s perspective, when he finally did agree to pay the doctor a visit, he was dismayed to discover that he should have done so long ago.

According to revue historian Haakon B. Nielson, as well as daughter Aud Schønemann's authorized biography, the comedian was found to suffer from pernicious anemia, an 'autoimmune illness' considered fatal at the time. First discovered and described thanks to the work of various physicists through the 19th century, pernicious anemia was much later found to be caused by vitamin B12 defficiency. In the early 1900s, people diagnosed with pernicious anemia were expected to live only up to three years after diagnosis. In the early 1920s, American physicist George Whipple performed testing on animals while doing research on the illness, and his findings suggested that devouring of raw liver could counteract anemia caused by chronic blood loss,[296] and so Whipple, along with colleagues of his, tried feeding raw liver daily to patients suffering from pernicious anemia, witnessing to their astonishment that said patients became fully rehabilitated within a couple of weeks. Regrettably, this revolutionary scientific finding was probably not something doctors in Norway could've been aware of in 1925. *If* indeed Schønemann did suffer from pernicious anemia – more on that below – it's *possible* that he would've been able to receive proper treatment for his condition, had he lived in the States.

A few weeks of rest at Holmenkollen sanatorium seemed to improve Schønemann's health, according to one report, and he «believed himself soon well enough to resume work» at Chat Noir.[297] He was driven home to the apartment of his dear sister Berthe Marie,[298] in Calmeyers gate 17 of central Kristiania, but sadly, the illness cast its grueling shadow over him once more. August Schønemann passed away at 9 o'clock A.M., February 18, 1925, surrounded by his closest family; exactly ten years after he'd first performed «his celebrated neutrality guard in the revue of 'Futt,' and instantly became the idol of the gallery.»[299]

Ovations were not long in coming. In the evening papers the very same day, as well as in papers the following morning, Schønemann's «rubberlike face» could be spotted practically everywhere across the nation. «Numerous are the roles he has portrayed in his career, and the people he has cheered number thousands,» mourned *Arbeiderbladet*. «[H]e wanted the best for all of us . . . remained always available and wished – as often as possible – to appear at the workers' gatherings. He felt that he belonged there.»[300]

«Krematoriet» – the Crematory, at Vestre Gravlund (Western Graveyard, Oslo) – could room only a small portion of the massive crowd which had shown up to pay their last respects. It has been said that literally thousands of people attended the comedian's funeral – yours truly has also been of this impression previously – but an exact number is probably impossible to affirm at this point. We do, however, know that «[e]very» theater venue of Oslo is said to have been represented, the hall adorned with bay laurels from Chat Noir. Kirsten Flagstad, the by now so famous soprano and, reportedly, a former sweetheart of the comedian, introduced the ceremony by performing the psalm *«Kjærlighet er lysets kilde»* («*Love is the Wellspring of Light*»), by Danish poet N. F. S. Grundtvig.

Newspaper photo from Schønemann's funeral, the auditorium being so crowded that most people, reportedly, had to stand outside. (Author's collection.)

The time came for the pastor to speak. «We stand at the end of a powerful lifespan,» he declared. Schønemann «possessed the gift of comedy, and lived it. He performed so well, equipped with a spark which set fire to a perennial spirit and bubbling energy. Speaking of his profession, one may cite the words of the great English predicant Spurgeon: 'I have never seen any harm be caused by making people laugh.'»

Following the speech, Flagstad again performed a song, «*I ensomme stunde*» («*In Lonely Moments*») by famous Norwegian composer and virtuoso Ole Bull, after which «a number of wreaths» were placed «on the catafalque», with silk ribbons signed Chat Noir, Casino, Theatre Moderne, Centraltheatret, and others. Finally, the Swedish comedy giant, Ernst Rolf, placed a wreath on the coffin, «in gratitude of loyal friendship.» Benno Singer and actor Victor Bernau served as Masters of ceremony.[301]

Records of Schønemann's songs were no doubt heard spinning across the country in succeeding weeks, months, and even years, but admirers of the phenomenal stage persona must have found this to be thin consolation. «Is Schønemann dead,» a cabdriver remarked to the actor's friend, Per Kvist. «Shall we never have any more *fun*, then?»[302]

A small, nameless boy was apparently of a more optimistic mindset: «Oh, think of all the fun *God*'ll have now!»[303]

Pernicious anemia?

As noted above, Haakon B. Nielson cites «pernicious anemia» as the illness which led to Schønemann's passing, and this is repeated in Aud's autobiography (1997), where it's assumed that he was diagnosed thus while hospitalized at the sanatorium, shortly before his final days. Yours truly also repeated this as the cause of

Schønemann's death, without hesitation, in the original, Norwegian version of this book. However, since then, the author has been able to view Schønemann's burial report in church books,[304] which gives tuberculosis as the cause of death. TB is given as the cause of Schønemann's death also in practically every newspaper notice in 1925 which yours truly has seen; at the time, the possibility of pernicious anemia seems not to have been brought up at all in the press.[305] As far as the author can tell, Nielson does not reveal his source when citing pernicious anemia as the cause of death, but, especially considering that Schønemann was diagnosed in the mid-1920s, it's perhaps not entirely implausible to think that doctors may have suspected both tuberculosis *and* pernicious anemia at some point, but eventually concluded TB to be the correct diagnosis. After all, severe tuberculosis often tends to result in symptoms similar to those associated with untreated pernicious anemia.

About two and a half years after Schønemann's passing, on October 31, 1927, a performance took place at the theater of Dovrehallen, with the aim of raising money for a memorial monument to be placed at his gravesite, made of black granite «in which a portrait relief of Schønemann, made by [sculptor] Morues,» would be «inserted».[306] Dovrehallen's stage was «beautifully decorated with laurel trees surrounding a relief of the artist» that night,[307] and speeches celebrating Schønemann both as a performer and human being were held – including one by Dovrehallen's director, who appears to have remarked that, ideally, this memorial performance should rather have been initiated «by the theater at which Schønemann was employed» (it's likely that the director here referred to Casino in particular). Although the auditorium was «full» that night, and the monument planned to be unveiled at Schønemann's gravesite the following February, it's not clear what came of it after the evening at Dovrehallen theater. For one reason or the other, the plans seem to have been shelved. (Nearly a century later, Schønemann's grandchild, Pål, tells the author that he'd never even heard of the plans of a memorial monument for Schønemann.[308])

Of Schønemann's sisters Anna, Agnes, and Berthe, he'd remained the closest to the latter, as the much older Anna and Agnes had moved from home when the comedian was still a child. After her brother's death in 1925, Berthe was hired at Centraltheatret (The Central Theater, later Oslo Nye Teater), officially as a «secretary», but she is said to have «filled capacities for which a theater usually requires 2 or 3 people».[309] Berthe was to survive all her siblings, passing away shortly before Christmas in 1968, aged 81.[310]

Kitty Normann, briefly married to Schønemann, remarried in 1926, to engineer Conrad Hopsdal, b. 1895; she is listed as «Kit*h*y Normann Schönemann» in the marriage register.[311] (Hopsdal had a daughter from a former marriage, Hellie Olga, who tragically died of tuberculosis at the age of six in 1927.)[312] The marriage with Conrad did not last, and in 1931, Kitty married a third time, to another engineer, Gustav Bernhard Myhre.[313] After marrying Gustav, Kitty seems to have retired from performing altogether. The couple remained married until Gustav's death at 54 in 1955.[314] Kitty passed away in March 1989, at nearly 93.[315] She seems to have led a mostly quiet life following her retirement, and the author does not know of any interviews done with her in later decades.

Bernhard Henry «Benno» Singer closed down Theatre Moderne only months after the passing of «his» great star, whereupon he left Norway for good. He died in Dublin in May 1934, aged 59. Actor, writer and *teatersjef* at Casino, Thorleif Klausen – responsible for writing Schønemann's first great success *Futt*, and so many of the comedian's succeeding productions – had passed away a couple of weeks before in Oslo. In the years after Theatre Moderne's shutdown and Benno Singer's departure, the vast amusement area of Christiania Tivoli experienced hard times. The entire quarter was finally closed down and torn apart in the mid-1930s, making way for the construction of Oslo's current City Hall – a venture which had been planned all the way back to 1916 – as well as several other, more «up-to-date» buildings.

The exterior of Casino theater still stands in the 2020s, however. The theater kept on going by the name of Casino until World War II, when the occupying forces shut it down and had it reopened as a Nazi propaganda theater. After the war, the place has gone under various names, currently «Christiania Theater» since 2007.

Schønemann's close friend, songwriter and fellow actor Per Kvist, wrote some of the most enduring comic songs of 20th century Norway in succeeding years. He passed away in 1947, aged 57.

Dagmar Kristensen and daughter Aud were «remembered with a piano and diamond ring» after the comedian's passing,[316] beyond various memorabilia which, with time, would give Aud an inkling of what a formidable celebrity her father had been, although they seldom talked about him at home. In 1931, Dagmar married photographer Ola Johansen,[317] whereupon she moved with the child to an apartment at Grønlandsleiret, Oslo.[318] (Aud recalled that, while she never referred to Ola as «Dad» or «father», she grew very fond of him.)

Rare are the instances when the child of a famous artist reaches heights comparable to the parent, but in Aud's case, this became the reality in the end, although it took its time to happen. In a radio interview from 1979, Aud recalled that she'd never «decided» to become a performer, per se. As her mother, Dagmar, had become an established performer by the time Aud was about three or four, Aud's own start as a performer just sort of «happened.»[319] (She never, according to herself, ever thought of becoming anything else, except perhaps for a brief time in childhood when she dreamed of working as a milkmaid.[320]) As such, Aud first made her mark while still a small child, in stagings of Sverre Brandt's beloved Christmas play,

Journey to the Christmas Star, in which she reappeared for several years.[321] At twenty, she was – like her father before her – hired as prompter, followed by various smaller parts, and larger supporting roles onstage from the late 1940s on. Around the same time, she married actor Jan Pande-Rolfsen, with whom she had the son Pål. (Aud and Jan remained married until Jan's passing 54 years later, in 2002.)

Aud Schønemann. 1969. (Nasjonalbiblioteket / The Norwegian National Library.)

By the early 1950s, Aud appeared in numerous productions and skits at Chat Noir, and achieved further recognition with appearances in the radio series *Søndagsposten* («*The Sunday Post*») later in the decade. However, despite being a performer of much experience by her 30s, Aud's rise to *stardom* was far more gradual than what had been the case with her father. Whereas August Schønemann's *breakthrough* had taken off with a bang, once he appeared in the revue of *Futt* at the age of 23, Aud was well into her 40s before reaching comparable fame. It was the comedy play, *Skulle det dukke opp flere lik er det bare å ringe («If Any More Bodies Turn Up, Let Us*

Know») in 1968 that made Aud, then aged 45, a national star in Norway. A huge moneymaker, in the play, Aud portrayed a nervous janitor who insists on having just seen a dead body, in the empty office building in which she works, but when the police arrives, the body is nowhere to be found. A similarly successful film version found its way onto the screen a couple of years later.

Hired at Oslo Nye Teater from 1968 to 1992, in addition to numerous tours and freelance jobs, Aud became an extremely beloved stage presence in Scandinavia, starring in an abundance of comedies and revues, and a few dramas as well, for three decades.

Rolv Wesenlund as 'Marve Fleksnes', Aud Schønemann playing his mother, 'Moder'n', from the TV series Fleksnes. *With this role, Aud probably reached her widest fame. Photo from the 1980s. (Nasjonalbiblioteket / The Norwegian National Library.)*

Today, Aud's enduring fame rests in particular on the portrayal of two recurring characters, one in film and one in TV, respectively. First, between 1969 and 1984, she appeared as «Valborg Jensen» in a total of 13 films, in the Norwegian *Olsenbanden* film comedy series (a final 14th film saw release in 1999). Based on a near-identical Danish film series, *Olsenbanden* (literally 'The Olsen Gang') centered on the escapades of three relatively harmless, if quite clumsy bandits always on the lookout for another big heist (which always failed in the end), «Valborg» being the nagging wife to one of the bandits. (In terms of humor, the film series can perhaps be compared to the *Pink Panther* films of the 1970s starring Peter Sellers, even though the slapstick elements of *Olsenbanden* generally played on a slightly less outrageous scale.) Although almost unanimously panned by critics at the time, the film series has remained arguably the most popular in Norway's history. In the aforementioned radio interview (1979), Aud stated of her participation in the *Olsenbanden* films: «I have so much *fun* in *Olsenbanden*. If the critics don't like the films, that can't be helped. We have a wonderful time doing them.»[322]

Even so, Aud probably reached her widest fame as the bossy mother in the TV comedy series *Fleksnes*, a Norwegian adaptation of the British TV series *Hancock's Half Hour*, written by Ray Galton and Allan Simpson. Starring Rolv Wesenlund as everyman and eternal bachelor «Marve Fleksnes», the *Fleksnes* series enjoyed immense popularity, not just in Norway, but in Sweden, Denmark, and Iceland, as well (it bears mentioning that it was considered an extreme rarity, at this time, for a Norwegian TV series to succeed anywhere outside of Norway). In the end, *Fleksnes* resulted in five 6-episode seasons shot between 1972 and 1982, as well as a full-length movie and a play (a sixth TV season, aired in 1988, mostly provided reruns of earlier episodes, coupled with new «vignette scenes»). The *Fleksnes* series' loyal director, Swedish-born Bo Hermansson, has revealed in later interviews that Aud's part in the series grew far more significant than what had been anyone's intention initially. Marve Fleksnes' mother was expected only to be a peripheral character in the series. Early on in *Fleksnes*, the main character was mostly accompanied by a wisecracking friend of his, very similar to the setup in *Hancock's Half*

Hour – but following a particularly successful shoot with Aud, director Hermansson reasoned that they may instead let *her*, as the mother, serve as «Marve Fleksnes'» persistent sidekick and «companion» in the series. As Hermansson has astutely observed, the dysfunctional, even slightly disturbing mother-son-relationship which thus evolved onscreen in succeeding episodes, gave *Fleksnes* a depth and dark undertone which was never really present in *Hancock*.[323]

Given that Norwegian households had access to just one single TV channel until into the 1980s, Aud's many TV appearances in these years passed few people by. Along with Rolv Wesenlund, she could, in fact, be rightfully described as one of the most famous, and *beloved*, performers of Northern Europe in the late 20th century.

Aud rarely spoke about her father, understandably so, given that she had no memories of him. In the aforementioned radio interview, she briefly remarked that «my father, of course, was actor August Schønemann, but of him I can't tell you anything, 'cause he passed away when I was two», and then hurriedly moved on.[324] The art of revue held a special place in Aud's heart, however. In a TV interview conducted by her colleague, Rolv Wesenlund, she stated: «I have such great respect for revue, it's one of the finest things I know! Standing there alone [onstage in a role], you must get everything done in just three minutes. . . . It's terribly hard to do. The role is just a 'sketch', but you have to do it *well*!»[325]

In 2001, years after the original *Fleksnes* TV series had ended, it was decided to produce one more *Fleksnes* episode to properly conclude the series, Aud reprising her role as «Marve Fleksnes»' mother. Preparing for a scene during this production, she joked (?) that she could «never tell what's supposed to be funny [in a scene], until people laugh.»[326] Aired around Christmas 2002, this turned out to be Aud's final performance, after which her health deteriorated. By the time of her passing in October 2006, at nearly 84, she had received numerous prestigious awards for her work, including The Amanda Commitee's Honorary Award (1997) and The Medal of St. Hallvard (2002), and even been appointed Knight 1st Class, Order of St. Olav. A statue of her, made by sculptor Nina Sundbye, was unveiled at the entrance of Oslo Nye Teater in 2010. Sundbye, who knew Aud personally, described her as a «wonderful human being, and magnificent performer.»[327]

Aud's mother, Dagmar, had passed away in 1987, at the age of 86.

Unfortunately, the Norwegian «golden age» of revue came to an end in the mid-20th century. Author and journalist Bjørn Brøymer has singled out the bankruptcy of comedian Leif Juster's revue theater, Edderkoppen ('The Spider'), in 1966 as a major contributor to the demise of Norwegian revue. «The so-called 'serious theaters' received public aid,» Brøymer explains, «but it wasn't proper to be funny.»[328]

(Even so, Norwegian revue was to experience a renaissance of sorts by the late 1960s, through the work of energetic, up-and-coming comedians such as Rolv Wesenlund and Harald Heide-Steen, Jr.[329] – at the time, Norway had arguably not seen such innovation in the art of revue since Chat Noir's production *Without a Thread* in 1924, starring August Schønemann.)

It may be futile to speculate on what heights August Schønemann would have reached, had he lived for just a few more years. So much time has now passed, that one easily forgets how tragically young he was upon his death; not yet 34 years old! We may mourn the fact that his filmography includes just one single title – and what's more, *no talking films* – but we may also listen with gratitude to the merry jargon that is preserved on records. One may also hope that a lost newsreel will eventually turn up, to provide us with some additional footage of the comedian; at the very least, such newsreels are rumored to have existed at one point.

It may, in fact, be possible that August Schønemann bid us farewell at the very peak of his career. By comparison, the Swedish revue king Ernst Rolf lived for another seven years, and ended his days in great economic worry; not due to a decreasing interest in *him* among the public, per se, but his splendid revues had difficulties covering their expenses once the Great Depression hit in.

When Ernst Rolf's life was made into a three-part mini-series in the early 1980s, produced by Swedish Television in cooperation with NRK (Norwegian Broadcasting), the role of August Schønemann was handed to Leif Jacobsen,[330] an actor mostly known from the stage. Jacobsen pulls off a decent performance as Schønemann, even though his time onscreen is sadly too brief for him to flesh out the portrayal as much as he may have been capable of. Opera singer Hans Josefsson did an enchanting, complex portrayal of Ernst Rolf, while Aud did a cameo appearance as a laundress. The mini-series took certain artistic liberties – we do, for instance, briefly spot «Schønemann» as a guest at Rolf's third wedding in 1930, which, of course, cannot have happened in reality – but it provides a colorful, lively depiction of the great revues of the 1920s. One wonders if some few, aging viewers, when the series aired around Christmas 1983 by the name of *Lykkeland*,[331] in their youth had seen the *real* August Schønemann and Ernst Rolf stir cheers and excitement at Casino, some sixty years before.

Notes

287. *Oslo Illustrerte*, No. 19, May 12, 1934.

288. Nielson, p. 54.

289. *Nå* magazine, #3/1959, pp. 20-21.

290. *Aftenposten*, evening edition, December 20, 1924, p. 13. Note: an American screen adaptation of *Little Miss Bluebeard* was made in 1925, starring Bebe Daniels, Robert Frazer and Raymond Griffith.

291. *Aftenposten*, morning edition, December 27, 1924, p. 4.

292. *Telemark Social-Demokrat*, December 23, 1924, p. 2.

293. *Aftenposten*, morning edition, January 13, 1925, p. 6.

294. *Arbeiderbladet*, February 11, 1925, p. 5.

295. Nielson, p. 54.

296. *George Hoyt Whipple / Biographical Memoirs V.66* (The National Academies Press), pp. 381-382.

297. *Arbeiderbladet*, February 18, 1925, p. 2.

298. *Folkets røst*, February 21, 1925, p. 2. See also Nielson.

299. *Aftenposten*, evening edition, February 18, 1925, p. 1.

300. *Arbeiderbladet*, February 18, 1925, p. 2.

301. *Aftenposten*, morning edition, February 25, 1925, p. 4.

302. *Humør 1932* (Kvist, Per), p. 150.

303. Gulbrandsen, Lars O., p. 23.

304. Burials: 1925-02-24. Church book from Jacob parish 1921-1948 (0301M7). (SAO, Jakob prestekontor Kirkebøker, SAO/A-10850/F/Fa/L0012 Parish register (official), no. 12, 1921-1948, p. 31.)

305. *Telemark Social-Demokrat*, February 19, 1925, p. 2. See also *Nidaros*, February 19, 1925, p. 3, and various other papers of the same week.

306. *Morgenbladet*, October 28, 1927, p. 3.

307. *Nationen*, November 1, 1927, p. 3.

308. Pål Pande-Rolfsen, correspondence with the author, 2022.

309. *Arbeiderbladet*, October 8, 1947, p. 2.

310. *Aftenposten*, morning edition, December 19, 1968, p. 17.

311. Marriage register (civil) for Bergen byfogd 1924-1927. (SAB, Byfogd og Byskriver i Bergen, 10F/10/L0003: Vielsesprotokoller, 1924-1927, p. 79.)

See also *Morgenavisen,* December 15, 1926, p. 4; and *Norsk Kunngjørelsestidende,* December 10, 1926, p. 1.

312. Church book from Oslo Domkirke / Vår Frelsers menighet parish 1919-1930 (0301M12). (Deceased and buried (1928) – SAO, Oslo domkirke Kirkebøker, SAO/A-10752/F/Fa/L0037Parish register (official) no. 37, 1919-1930, p. 196.) See also Church book from the Norwegian Seamen's Mission in Antwerp, Belgium 1914-1930 (3602). (Burials: 1927-03-29.) Note: It seems that Hopsdal's daughter Hellie/Helly passed away in Belgium, although a funeral ceremony was held in Norway the following year.

313. Church book from Nykirken parish 1926-1934. Marriages: 1931-10-17. (SAB, Nykirken Sokneprestembete, SAB/A-77101/H/Haa/L0038Parish register (official) no. D 8, 1926-1934, p. 103b-104a.)

314. *Bergens Tidende,* June 1, 1955, p. 11.

315. *Bergens Arbeiderblad,* April 1, 1989, p. 33.

316. Gulbrandsen, Lars O., p. 24.

317. Marriages: 1931-08-08. Church book from Østre Aker parish 1914-1936 (0218bP). SAO, Østre Aker prestekontor Kirkebøker, SAO/A-10840/G/Ga/L0004 Parish register (copy) no. I 4, 1914-1936, p. 503-504.) Note: Ola Johansen seems to have been listed as "Ole" in the marriage register, but he is consistently referred to as "Ola" in Aud's autobiography.

318. Gulbrandsen, Lars O., pp. 27-28.

319. Radio interview with Aud Schønemann. NRK. June 1979.

320. Ibid.

321. Gulbrandsen, Lars O., p. 24.

322. Radio interview with Aud Schønemann. NRK. June 1979. Incidentally, rehearsals and interior shots for the *Olsenbanden* films generally took place in a small film studio at Keysergate 1, Oslo, almost right across the Trinity

Church where Aud's paternal grandparents, August Pettersen Sr. and Thrine Josefine Pettersen, had given their vows in 1874.

323. Lind, Kalle (podcast): *Snedtänkt*. «Om Bosse Hermansson.» March 19, 2019.

324. Radio interview with Aud Schønemann. NRK. June 1979.

325. TV interview with Aud Schønemann. NRK. April 5, 1972.

326. TV news broadcast (Dagsrevyen). NRK. September 2001.

327. NRK, article / Web reportage. October 21, 2010.

328. *Aftenposten*, December 8, 2010.

329. Hegge, Per Egil: *Rolv Wesenlund ... og takk for det!* (Juritzen forlag, 2014), pp. 79-92.

330. Sadly, Jacobsen was to pass away in 1986 at the age of 46, due to heart failure. See *Drammens Tidende og Buskeruds blad*, January 27, 1986, p. 3.

331. Not to be confused with a Norwegian TV series by the same name produced in 2018, a dramatization of the events leading up to Norway becoming an «oil nation» in the 1970s.

Selected stage chronology

It would probably be impossible to list all stage appearances by August Schønemann, from his acting debut in 1906 up to his passing in 1925. I have here listed a selection of important stage appearances from 1906—1914; all his known revue appearances at Theatre Moderne 1915—1924; as well as all of his known appearances in plays, operettas and revues at Casino (1921—24) and Chat Noir (1924—25).

1906

Østre Theater (Eastern Theater – Grønlandsleiret, Kristiania): 1-act play *Portnerens plageånder* ('Tormented Janitor'), small part.

1907

February 16: 1-act play *Ingvald Enersen* (as police officer); 1-act play *Til Sæters* ('To the Moutain Pastures', as a student); both at the Student Society of Kristiania.

Performed comic songs at Vestre Teater (Western Theater), Bogstadvn. 12, Kristiania.

?On tour with *Oliver Twist* (dir. Jacob von der Lippe); Schønemann's involvement disputed, possible small part. Tour lasted fall 1907—spring 1908.

1908

November 27: 1-act play *Onkels Kjærlighed* ('Lovestruck Uncle', as rentier); 1-act rendition of *Charley's Aunt*; both in Kristiansund, Norway.

1909—1914

March 7 – late April 1909: signed contract with Det norske Teaterselskab (The Norwegian Theater Company), appearing at Drammen Theater (suburb nearby Kristiania) each Sunday, in plays such as *Wærmlændingerne* (March 14; 6 acts), and *Andersen, Pettersen, Lundstrøm*. Performed in Ludvig Holberg's *Jeppe on the Hill* (Tønsberg, April 18; Drammen, May 4).

August 9, 1909 – August 30, 1911: served as prompter at Fahlstrøm's Theater, Kristiania. Stayed with Fahlstrøm until the theater's 'farewell performance' in late summer 1911. Also received roles onstage during his time there, in plays such as *Quo Vadis?*, *A Chinese Honeymoon*, *Zigeunerliebe*, and *Fall Maneuver.*

October 1911 – May 1912: signed contract at Pehr Qværnstrøm's Folk Theater, Kristiania. Went on tour across the country with the Folk Theater that fall. Performed in various plays, such as Ludvig Müller's *Den nye lensmanden* ('The New Sheriff'); *Det uhyggelige Portræt* ('The Gruesome Portrait'); *Spøgelseshuset* ('The Haunted House', Schønemann as 'rentier Silberstein', one of his first major roles); *Det gjør ingenting* ('It Doesn't Matter'); *The Telegram* ('Telegrammet'); *Jeppe paa Bjerget* ('Jeppe on the Hill'); *Svigermor! Pas Paa!* ('Mother-In-Law! Be Careful!'); *Hittebarnet* ('The Orphan'); *Paa Dydens Vei* ('Virtue's Path'); *Kvindelist* ('Cunning Women'); and *Ægtemandens Representant* ('The Husband's Representative').

June 1, 1912 – August 1912: engaged at the 'Summer Theater of Kongsberg' by Pehr Qværnstrøm.

August 1912 – summer 1913: teamed up with actor Paul Magnussen onstage; details largely unclear. At least assumed to have appeared with Magnussen at Cirkus Verdensteater (Circus World Theater) of Kristiania during spring 1913.

June 1913 – August 1913: again engaged at the 'Summer Theater of Kongsberg' by Qværnstrøm.

October 1913 – April/May 1914: hired at Tivoli Theater (of Christiania Tivoli), appeared in plays such as the French comedy *73 Champignol*; Bayard Veiller's drama *Within the Law*; and the comedy *Lys over land* ('Light Over Land').

July 16 – August 1914: appeared at Tivolihaven (outdoors facility for summer entertainment at Christiania Tivoli) in Paul Magnussen's 2-act «Anniversary Revue», *Skum* ('Foam').

September – October 1914: went on tour with Paul Magnussen in several Norwegian towns (Rjukan and Sarpsborg in October), performed revue.

Revue appearances at Theatre Moderne (1915—1924).

Futt.
['Futt'; informal Norwegian phrase for high energy.]
Written by Thorleif Klausen, Michael Flagstad.
Performed February 18, 1915 – April 16, 1915.
Total of 60 performances.
Schønemann as Professor Jo Vellesen; a cop; a frozen soldier.

Sort paa hvidt, a.k.a. **Kristiania Mosaik.**
['Black on White'; a.k.a. 'Kristiania Mosaic.']
Written by Thorleif Klausen.
Performed November 16, 1915 – February 1916.
Schønemann in various roles.

Razzia.
['Raids.']
Written by Thorleif Klausen.
Performed March 1916 – April 1916.
Schønemann in various roles; played opposite Josef Sjøgren's «Charlie Chaplin»-impersonation.

Mammon.
['Mammon.']
Written by Thorleif Klausen.
Performed October 16, 1917 – December 14, 1917.
Total of 60 performances.
Cast: August Schønemann («shipowner Peder Mikkelsen»); Kitty Normann; numerous others.

Nyttaarsrevy – Dusch.
['New Year's Revue – Dusch.']
Written by Thorleif Klausen.
Performed January 1, 1918 – February 1918.
Schønemann playing «unemployed police officer», among other roles.

Nyttaarsrevy – Paa stedet hvil.
['New Year's Revue – At Ease.']
Written by Thorleif Klausen.
Performed January 1, 1919 – April 27, 1919.
Total of 115 performances.

Schønemann as frightened soldier, among other roles.

Caviar.
['Caviar.']
Written by Thorleif Klausen.
Performed March 13, 1919 – May 14, 1919.
Schønemann in the double role of a hotel manager and piccolo.

Dit og dat.
['This and That.']
Written by Thorleif Klausen.
Performed November 1, 1919 – December 31, 1919.
Total of 60 performances.
Cast: August Schønemann; Max Hansen; numerous others.

Nyttaarsrevy – Tak! I lige maade!
['New Year's Revue – Thanks, Same to You!']
Written by Thorleif Klausen.
Performed January 1, 1920 – March 1920.
Schønemann in various roles.

Paa'n igjen – fra Vippetangen til Honolulu.
['Here We Go Again – from Vippetangen(*) to Honolulu.']
Written by Thorleif Klausen.
Performed March 17, 1920 – May 13, 1920.
Cast: August Schønemann; Max Hansen; Lilly Grimsgaard; numerous others.
(*)Vippetangen; southern tip of the peninsula in central Oslo.

Overalls.
['Overalls.']
Written by Thorleif Klausen.
Performed November 1, 1920 – February 27, 1921.

Cast: August Schønemann (as «tailor M. F. Traadsby», meaning «Threadtown»); Lilly Grimsgaard; Aasta Heide; Thorleif Michelsen; numerous ballet dancers.

Galla Petter.
['White Tie Petter.']
Written by «Pjerre & Co» (writing team).
Performed January 1, 1921 – March 1921.
Schønemann in various roles.

Snip, snap, snute.
['Snipp, snapp, snute'; Norwegian phrase usually used to mark the end of a fairytale – 'the end of the road', 'they lived happily ever after.']
Written by «Pjerre & Co» (writing team).
Performed March 23, 1921 – April 24, 1921.
Included sketch of Schønemann embarking on a «voyage» to America.

Kvinden du gav mig midt i planeten.
['The Woman You Threw Right in My Head.']
Written by «Filnis Cometi & Co» (writing team).
Performed October 31, 1922 – December 31, 1922.
Schønemann in guest appearance.

Storting og smaating.
['Parliament & Little Things'; literal translation.]
Written by «Lyktemanden» (pseudonym).
Performed January 19, 1923 – ?April 13, 1923.
Schønemann starred as «Emperor Wilhelm II».

Cirkus Christiania. [NB – actually staged at Casino theater, although under the banner of Theatre Moderne.]
['Circus Christiania.']

Written by ?
Performed May 29, 1924 (Schønemann joined June 12) – August 1924.
Schønemann playing «inventor Sæbædius Rukke», guest appearance.

Appearances at Casino theater (1921—1924), plays, operettas, revues.

Damen paa Nr. 23.
['The Woman at Room 23.']
8 acts. Written by Paul Gavaul.
Performed September 10, 1921 – November 1921.
Cast: Conrad Arnesen; Signe Heide-Steen; August Schønemann; Thorleif Klausen.

Den evige lampe.
['The Eternal Lamp.']
3 acts. Written by Otto Härting.
Performed December 14, 1921 – March 5, 1922.
Cast: Fredrik Wingar; Agnes Lind; Trine Bull; Nora Ulleberg; Conrad Arnesen; August Schønemann.

Loppen i øret.
['A Flea in Her Ear.']
3 acts. Written by Georges Feydeau.
Performed January 10, 1922 – March 1922.
Cast: Jens Hetland; Thorleif Klausen; August Schønemann (as Feraillon); numerous others.

Mr. Jazz.
Revue. 3 acts. Written by Thorleif Klausen.
Performed March 4, 1922 – May 21, 1922.
Includes installment about a trip "across the globe."

Schønemann in various roles; Klausen and Conrad Arnesen also appeared, among others.

Fru Postmester.
['The Postmistress.']
3 acts. Written by August Neidhart; Léol Jessel (music).
Performed April 30, 1922 – May 27, 1922.
Cast: Otti Pegel; Harald Aimarsen; Conrad Arnesen; August Schønemann.

Reservebaronen.
['The Imaginary Baron.']
Written by «Pordes-Milo»; Hermann Haller; Walter Kollo (music).
Performed June 5, 1922 – April 8, 1923 (intermission at Casino July—August 1923; performed at the Summer theater of Fredrikstad during these months).
Cast: Fredrik Wingar; Ebba Toje; Conrad Arnesen; August Schønemann.

Jorden rundt i 80 dage.
['Around the World in 80 Days.']
Based on the novel by Jules Verne; adaptation by Erik Bøgh.
Performed April 27, 1923 – June 26, 1923.
Cast: Jens Selmer (Phileas Fogg); August Schønemann (Passepartout); Thorleif Klausen (Detective Fix).

Fra Karl Johan til Lykkeland.
['From the Street of Karl Johan to Paradise.']
Revue. Various writers.
Performed July 1, 1923 – October 28, 1923.
Total of 128 performances.
Cast: Ernst Rolf; August Schønemann (Alfred the lion tamer, among other roles); Signe Heide-Steen (later replaced by Ebba Toje); numerous others.

Prins Don Juan.
['Prince Don Juan.']
Written by Karl Thiemann; Hans Planter; Victor Corzilius (music).
Performed October 30, 1923 – December 16, 1923.
Cast: Ragnar Wingar; Thorleif Klausen; August Schønemann; numerous others.

Mikadoen.
['The Mikado.']
Written by Arthur Sullivan (music); W. S. Gilbert (libretto).
Directed by Max Reinhardt.
Performed December 26, 1923 – February 8, 1924.
Total of 45 performances.
Cast: Conrad Arnesen (Nanki-Poo); Aslaug Mühlenphort-Ohldick (Yum-Yum); August Schønemann (Ko-Ko); Harald Aimarsen.

Grand Hotel Amor.
['Grand Hotel Amor.']
3 acts. Written by Leo Kestner; Hans H. Zerlett; Siegfried Schultz (music).
Performed February 10, 1924 – May 17, 1924.
Cast: Thorleif Klausen (hotel manager); August Schønemann (Conny Twinkel); Conrad Arnesen; Borghild Lykke; Sigrun Svenningsen; Lilly Andersen; Trine Bull; Kätie Rolfsen; Alf Sommer.

Kaptein Grants barn.
['In Search of the Castaways.']
Based on the novel by Jules Verne.
Performed April 26, 1924 – June 7, 1924.
Cast: Thorleif Klausen (Captain Grant); August Schønemann (Paganel); Signe Heide-Steen; Trine Bull; Sigrun Svenningsen; Nora Ulleberg; Conrad Arnesen; Idar Trana.

Appearances at Chat Noir (1924—1925), one revue, one play.

Uten en traad.
['Without a Thread.']
Revue. Written by Arne Svendsen; Per Kvist.
Performed September 1, 1924 – ?January 11, 1925.
Cast: August Schønemann (a barber; Hamlet; among other roles); Lalla Carlsen (Ophelia); Victor Bernau; Henrik Dahl; Per Kvist; Märtha Reiners, Botten Soot.

Vor lille frue.
['Little Miss Bluebeard.']
3 acts. Written by Avery Hopwood.
Performed December 11, 1924 (Kristiania première December 26) – March 29, 1925 (Schønemann replaced permanently by Josef Sjøgren c. January 13).
Cast: Kirsten Monrad-Aas; Victor Bernau; August Schønemann; Märta Reiners; Einar Vaage; Henrik Dahl; Josef Sjøgren (from Jan. 1925).

Filmography

1922

Kjærlighet paa Pinde – En sommerspøk.

['Love on a Stick – A Summer Prank,' literal translation. 'Lollipop.']
4 reels (44 min.). Silent. Tinted, B/W.
Shot and produced May—July 1922.
Released September 4, 1922, at Admiral Palads (later Eldorado
Kino), Torvgt. 9. Kristiania (now Oslo), Norway.
Screenplay, director: Erling Eriksen.
Photography (uncredited): Erling R. Knudsen.
Scenography, technical consultant (uncredited): Leif Sinding.
Produced and distributed by: Skandinavisk Filmcentral.
Cast: August Schønemann; Eva Sinding; Conrad Arnesen.

Bibliography

BOOKS

Bang-Hansen, Odd: *Chat Noir og Norsk Revy* (J.W. Cappelens forlag, 1961)

Baker, Richard Anthony: *British Music Hall – An Illustrated History* (Sutton Publishing, 2005)

Bernau, Victor; Klausen, Thorleif; Kvist, Per; (etc): *Humør 1932* (Aschehoug, 1932)

Borgen, Johan: *De mørke kilder* (Den norske Bokklubben, 1989; first published 1956).

Bødtkers, Sigurd: *Kristiania-premiérer gjennem 30 aar* (H. Aschehoug & Co., 1929)

Engelstad, Carl Fredrik: *Ludvig Holberg – Gjøgleren. Granskeren. Gåten.* (Aschehoug, 1984)

Gulbrandsen, Lars O.: *Aud Schønemann – Det blir mellom oss* (Se og Hør Forlaget, 1997)

Hansen, Halvard Normann: *En bok om film og kino ved Sarpsborg kommunale kinematografers 50-års jubileum* (Frank Vardings Trykkeri, Sarpsborg, 1965)

Hayes, Kevin J. (editor): *Charlie Chaplin Interviews* (University Press of Mississippi, 2005)

Heltberg, A. H. (editor): *Norsk film gjennom 35 år* (Centralforlaget, 1943)

Heltberg, A. H.: *Muntre Minner fra Norsk Teaterliv* (Norden Forlag, 1944)

Hegge, Per Egil: *Rolv Wesenlund ... og takk for det!* (Juritzen forlag, 2014)

Herresdahl, Harald (etc): *Norsk operafest: Norsk operakunst gjennom 200 år* (Lobo Grafisk AS, 1998)

Jensen, Magnus: *Norges Historie – Under eneveldet 1660-1814* (Universitetsforlaget Oslo – Bergen, 1962)

Jensen, Magnus: *Norges Historie – Unionstiden 1814-1905* (Universitetsforlaget Oslo – Bergen, 1963)

Jensen, Magnus: *Norges Historie – Fra 1905 til våre dager* (Universitetsforlaget Oslo – Bergen, 1965)

Hagen, Kai (editor): *Byen vår – Glimt av Oslo gjennom 900 år* (Herman Ruuds forlag, 1948)

Kindem, Ingeborg Eckhoff: *Den norske operas historie* (Ernst G. Mortensen – Forlagsavdelingen, 1941)

Kvist, Per: *Når katten er ute... – Chat Noir 1912-1942* (Det Mallingske Boktrykkeri, 1942)

Madsen, Birger: *Arbeiderforeningens Teater – Tivoli og Tivoli-Haven, Lokal Teaterhistorie 1875-1939* (Næsgaards Boktrykkeri, 1975)

Meidal, Björn: *God dag, mitt barn! – Berättelsen om August Strindberg, Harriet Bosse och deras dotter Anne-Marie* (Albert Bonniers Förlag, 2002)

Michelet, Marte: *Den største forbrytelsen – Ofre og gjerningsmenn i det norske Holocaust* (Gyldendal, 2014)

Nicolaysen, N.: *Bergens Borgerborg. 1: 1550-1751* (Werner & Co.s Bogtrykkeri, 1878)

Nielson, Haakon B.: *Revystjerner i 1920-årenes Kristiania* (J.W. Cappelens Forlag AS, 1970)

Randen, Olav: *Brøyte seg til rydning – Bureisingstid og bureisarliv* (Boksmia forlag, 2002)

Rein, Aslaug: *Kirsten Flagstad* (Ernst G. Mortensens Forlag, 1967)

Robinson, David: *Chaplin – His Life and Art* (Paladin Grafton Books, 1985)

Rose, Einar: *Rose-boka*. Ernst G. Mortensens forlag, 1941)

Rønneberg, Anton: *Skuespillerinnen Tore Segelcke* (H. Aschehoug & Co., 1946)

Sandvik, O.M., Schjelderup, Gerh. (editors): *Norges musikhistorie* (Vol. II), (Eberh. B. Oppi Kunstforlag, 1921)

Surgenor, Douglas M.: *Edwin J. Cohn and the Development of Protein Chemistry* (The Center for Blood Research & Harvard Medical School, 2002)

Ødegaard, Jac R.: *Slagerboka – Populærmusikkens historie gjennom 200 år* (Tempo forlag A/S, 1953).

Papers / Magazines

Various issues of *1ste Mai, Aftenposten, Akershus Social- Demokrat, Arbeiderbladet, Arbeider-Politikken, Bergens Tidende, Christiania Intelligentssedler, Dagbladet, Daggry, Den 17de Mai, Flekkefjords-Posten, Fredrikstad Tilskuer, Fremtiden, Hedemarkens Amtstidende, Kongsberg Dagblad, Middagsavisen, Morgenbladet, Morgenposten, Moss Tilskuer, Nationen, Nidaros, Norsk Kundegjø- relsestidende, Oslo Illustrerte, Port Huron Times-Herald, Ringerikes Blad, Romsdals Amtstidende, Social-Demokraten, Smaalenes Social- Demokrat, Telemark Social-Demokrat, Trondhjems Adresseavis, Tvedestrandsposten, Tyrihans, Tønsbergs Blad, Vestfold Arbeider- blad* and *Vårt Land*. Also *St. Hallvard: Illustrert tidsskrift for byhistorie, miljø og debatt* (2015, Vol. 93, No. 4).

Podcasts

Carlin, Dan: *Hardcore History 50 – Blueprint for Armageddon I* (October 29, 2013).

Lind, Kalle: *Snedtänkt*. «Om Bosse Hermansson» (March 19, 2019).

Radio

Interview with Aud Schønemann (NRK). June 1979.

TV

Kjære kollega (NRK), episode 1, April 1972. Interview with Aud Schønemann.

Si det som det er! (NRK), November 13, 1976. Interview with Leif Juster.

Lykkeland (SVT, NRK, MTV3), 1983. Mini-series dramatization of the life of Ernst Rolf.

Websites

Www.aftenposten.no

www.digitalarkivet.no

www.nb.no

www.nrk.no

www.sceneweb.no

www.slektogdata.no

Various

Census 1865 for 0203B Drøbak prestegjeld, Drøbak kjøpstad. Arkivref. RA/S-2231.

Census 1875 for 0301 Kristiania kjøpstad. Arkivref. RA/S- 2231/E.

Census 1900 for 0301 Kristiania kjøpstad. Arkivref. RA/S- 2231/E.

Census 1910 for 0301 Kristiania kjøpstad. Arkivref. RA/S- 2231/E/ Ef..

Garnisonsmenigheten Kirkebøker (Parish register), G7Ga/L0002: Klokkerbok nr. 2, 1810-1814.

Nesodden prestekontor Kirkebøker (Parish register), F/Fa/L0007: Ministerialbok nr. I 7, 1848-1968.

SAO, Uranienborg prestekontor Kirkebøker (Parish register), SAO/ A-10877/F/Fa/L0012Ministerialbok nr. 12, 1914-1930, p. 92.

(For more church books / parish registers, please see Notes section.)

"Theater-Bog! August Schønemann – 9 april 1909." August Schønemann's personal scrapbook, stored at the Norwegian National Library.

About the Author

Snorre Smári Mathiesen is author of the book *Max Linder: Father of Film Comedy* (published by BearManor Media, 2017), and creator of the independently-published comic book series *Dretzel & Marcel*, available on Amazon.com. He has studied art, and otherwise prefers to spend his time on such things as listening to Jack Benny's radio show, or reading George Herriman's *Krazy Kat*. He lives in Oslo, Norway.

Index

Generally speaking, the Index is systematized such that the *revues* use their original, Norwegian titles, whereas *plays* rely on English titles.

Aabel, Hauk, 45, 48, 53, 165

Aabel, Per, 45

Adolphsdatter, Berthe Marie (paternal great-grandmother), 19

Arbuckle, Roscoe C., 120

Arnesen, Conrad, 106, 111, 121, 123, 130, 131, 160, 161, 194-198

Around the World in 80 Days, 147, 148, 162, 195

At Ease! (revue), see *Paa stedet hvil*

Auntie Bag (1940), 131

Beethoven, Ludwig van, 52

Belle Époque, La (period), 107

Benny, Jack, 38

Bernau, Victor, 60, 163, 164, 172, 175, 197

Bernick, Georg, 51

Black on White (revue), see *Sort paa hvidt*

Bodanzky, Robert, 48

Bonaparte, Napoléon, 13

Bøgh, Erik, 147, 195

Book-Jensen, Jens, 163

Bosse, Harriet, 44

Brandt, Sverre, 178

Brun, Johannes, 27

Bull, Ole, 175

Campbell, Herbert, 29

Cantor, Eddie, 7

Carlsen, Lalla, 165-167, 171, 197

Carmen (opera), 90

Casino (theater), 103-113, 120, 121, 130, 131, 137, 147-150, 156, 158-164, 171, 175-178, 184, 193, 194-196

Caught in a Cabaret (1914), 118

Caviar (revue), 94, 195

Chaplin, Charlie, 7, 41, 65, 80-81, 118, 120, 122, 127, 145, 172, 191

Chaplin, Sydney, 38, 145

Charley's Aunt, 37-38, 98-99,
   116, 189
Chat Noir (theater), 31, 164-
   167, 170-175, 179, 183,
   196-197
Chekhov, Anton, 41
Chinese Honeymoon, A, 46-48,
   189
Christian VI (Dan.-Norw. king),
   29
Christian VII (Dan.-Norw.
   king), 13
Christiania Tivoli, 8, 31, 61-63,
   66-67, 91, 97, 103, 135, 177,
   190
Circus Christiania (revue), 163,
   193
Coborn, Charles, 29
Corzilius, Victor, 158, 195
Count, The (1916), 118
Crosby, Bing, 163
Damen paa Nr. 23 (play), see
   Woman at Room 23, The
Dance, George, 46
*Dangers in a Fisherman's Life, A
   Drama on the Sea* (c. 1908),
   119
Deed, André, 45
Den evige lampe (play), see
   Eternal Lamp, The
Desvallières, Maurice, 62
Dit og Dat (*This and That*,
   revue), 97-98

Drangsholt, Erling, 134
Dreyer, Carl Th., 120
duel de Max, Le (1913), 122
Dusch (revue), 90, 191
Dybwad, Jacob, 150
Egede-Nissen, Aud (later
   Richter), 135
Eriksen, Erling, 120-121, 128,
   131
Eternal Lamp, The (play), 107,
   194
Fahlstrøm, Alma, 43-44, 48-49
Fahlstrøm, Johan, 43-44, 46,
   48-49, 56
Fairhair, Harald, 12
Fall Maneuver, 47-48, 189
Fall, Leo, 45
Feydeau, Georges, 62, 107
*Fiskerlivets farer - Et drama på
   havet* (c. 1908), see *Dangers
   in a Fisherman's Life, A
   Drama on the Sea*
Flagstad, Kirsten, 51-52, 58-59,
   104, 174, 175
Flagstad, Michael, 68
Flea in Her Ear, A (play), 107,
   194
Fleksnes (TV series), 180,
   181-182
Fra Karl Johan til Lykkeland
   (revue), 149-150, 156, 158, 195
Frederic III (Dan.-Norw. king),
   13

Frederic V (Dan.-Norw. king), 29

Frederic VI (Dan.-Norw. king), 13

From Karl Johan to Paradise, see *Fra Karl Johan til Lykkeland*

Fru postmester (play), see *Postmistress, The*

Futt (revue), 68-75, 78, 79, 81, 88, 102, 150, 173, 177, 179, 190

Galla Petter (revue), 101, 193

Geijerstam, Gustaf af, 45

Gerhardsen, Einar, 141

Gilbert, W. S., 159, 196

Gitowsky, Michael, 94

Grand Hotel Amor (play), 161, 196

Grieg, Edvard, 11

Grimsgaard, Lilly, 101, 102, 192, 193

Growth of the Soil (novel), 120

Grundtvig, N. F. S. (poet), 174

Haakon VII (Norwegian king), 14, 21

Hamilton, Lloyd, 132

Hamlet (character), 41, 166-167

Hamsun, Knut, 120

Hancock's Half Hour, 181-182

Hannevig, Christoffer, 104

Hansen, Max, 97, 98, 192

Hardrada, Harald, 12

Henie, Sonja, 11

Here We Go Again (revue), see *Paa'n igjen*

Hermansson, Bo, 181-182

Hitler, Adolf, 145

Holberg, Ludvig, 29, 39, 51, 189

Hopwood, Avery, 172, 197

Høstmanøver, see *Fall Maneuver*

Ibsen, Henrik, 11, 41

If Any More Bodies Turn Up, Let Us Know (play), see *Skulle det dukke opp flere lik, er det bare å ringe*

Imaginary Baron, The (play), 111-113, 195

In Search of the Castaways, 161-163, 168, 196

Jacobsen, Leif (actor), 184, 187

Jeppe on the Hill, 39, 51, 189

Jessel, Léol, 111, 193

Jitney Elopement, A (1915), 118

Johansen, Ola (photographer), 178

Jolson, Al, 7, 8, 133

Josefsson, Hans, 184

Journey to the Christmas Star (play), 179

Juster, Leif, 139, 183

Kastner, Leo, 161

Katzenjammer Kids, The (comic strip), 28

Kaufman, Philip, 140

Keaton, Buster, 122, 127

Kid, The (1921), 122

Kjærlighet paa Pinde (1922), 18, 106, 119-133, 137, 141, 170, 198

Klausen, Thorleif, 68, 69, 73, 87, 88, 94, 97, 101, 105, 106, 110, 130-131, 137, 147, 148, 158, 160-162, 177, 190-191, 193, 195-196

Knudsen, Erling R., 126

Knudsen, Gunnar (Norw. prime minister), 89

Kollo, Walter, 111

Kristensen, Dagmar, 134-136, 142, 161, 178, 183

Kvinden du gav mig midt i planeten (revue), 137, 193

Kvinnsland, Andreas, 103

Kvist, Per, 106, 114, 131, 137, 151, 161, 164, 175, 178, 197

Lehár, Franz, 48

Linder, Max, 45, 120, 121

Lippe, Jakob von der, 33, 36

Little Miss Bluebeard (play), 172, 174, 197

Lloyd, Harold, 120, 122, 123, 127

Loppen i øret, see *Flea in Her Ear, A*

Lyche, Borghild, 105

Lykkeland (1983 mini-series), 184

Magnussen, Paul, 56-58, 62-63, 64, 77-78, 79, 80, 82-83, 90, 190

Mammon (revue), 88-90, 99, 191

Markens grøde (novel), see *Growth of the Soil*

Max's Duel (1913), see *duel de Max, Le* (1913)

Max veut apprendre à patiner (1907), 45

Mikado, The (play), 159-161, 196

Monrad Aas, Kirsten, 172

Mr. Jazz (revue), 110

Müller, Ludvig, 50

Murder Without a Face (1936), 131

Nielsen, Asta, 78, 80, 83

Nielson, Haakon B., 9, 29, 33, 46, 49, 52, 57, 59, 67, 68, 75, 93, 107, 108, 140, 163, 172, 175, 176

Normann, Kitty, 90, 91-92, 94, 99, 102, 105, 109, 134, 135, 161, 177, 191

Oliver Twist, 33, 188

Olsenbanden (film series), 181, 186

Opera Comique (theater), 103-105

Ophelia (character), 166, 167

Opsahl, Arve, 137

Orphans, The (1939), 131

Oselio, Gina, 90

Østbye, Adolf, 30

Overalls (revue), 7, 100-101, 192-193

Paa stedet hvil (revue), 94, 191

Paa'n igjen (revue), 98, 192

Pande-Rolfsen, Jan, 177

Pande-Rolfsen, Pål, 9, 177

Pathé (film studio), 46

Pedersen, Karl (actor), 63

Pegel, Otti, 111, 195

Pettersen, Agnes Mathea Johanna (sister), 22, 25, 26, 41, 68, 177

Pettersen, Anna Augusta Maranda (sister), 22, 41, 68, 177

Pettersen, August Sr. (father), 10, 18-22, 38, 62, 64, 84, 187

Pettersen, Berthe Marie (Schønemann-Nielsen) (sister), 21, 22, 68, 83, 173, 177

Pettersen, Birger Olaf Johannes (brother), 22, 25

Pettersen, Olaf (brother), 22

Pettersen, Thrine Josefine (b. Engebretsen, mother), 18-22, 68, 76, 187

Pink Panther, The (film series), 181

Poincaré, Raymond, 146

Porat, Otto von, 108-109

Postmistress, The (play), 111, 194

Prince Don Juan (play), 158, 159, 195-196

Quo Vadis?, 46, 189

Qværnstrøm, Pehr, 49-54, 56, 58, 59, 79, 189, 190

Razzia (revue), 80-81, 191

Reiners, Märta, 164, 197

Reinhardt, Max, 159-160, 196

Reisen til Julestjernen (play), see *Journey to the Christmas Star*

Relph, Harry "Little Tich", 30

Reservebaronen (play), see *Imaginary Baron, The*

Right Stuff, The (1983), 140

Riis, Claus Pavels, 34

RMS *Titanic* (passenger liner), 48

Roaring Twenties (period), 109

Rolf, Ernst, 32-33, 80, 120, 137-140, 149-150, 159, 175, 184, 195

Rolf, Tom, 140

Sailor-Made Man, A (1921), 123

Saint-Säens, Camille, 104

Schanche, Ingolf, 166

Schjønneman, Jonathan Fredrik (paternal great-grandfather), 19

Schjønnemann Pettersen, Frithjof Jens (brother), 22, 26

Schjønneman/Schøneman, August Frederik (paternal grandfather), 19

Schønemann, Aud (daughter), 18, 56, 135-137, 161, 172, 175, 178-183

Scorsese, Martin, 140

Segelcke, Tore, 98-99

Sellers, Peter, 181

Sennett, Mack, 121, 122, 129

Shoulder Arms (1918), 145

Sinding, Ellen, 121, 123, 124, 170

Sinding, Leif, 120-121, 131-132, 170-171, 198

Singer, Bernhard Henry "Benno", 61, 63, 65-67, 68, 69, 73-74, 77, 78, 79, 80, 81, 88, 90, 93, 102, 103, 104, 105, 106, 137, 163, 175, 177

Sjøgren, Josef, 81, 172, 191, 197

Sjöström, Victor, 120

Skandinavisk Filmcentral, 120, 130

Skram, Amalie, 50

Skulle det dukke opp flere lik er det bare å ringe (play), 179-180

Snip, snap, snute (revue), 102, 193

Soot, Ingeborg "Botten", 165, 171

Sort paa hvidt (revue), 98, 99, 101, 102, 248

Spurgeon, Charles, 175

Steen, Harald Heide, 94

Steen, Johannes, 27

Steen, Signe Heide, 94, 106, 150-151, 170, 194-195

Storting og Smaating (revue), 145-146, 147, 193

Strindberg, August, 41, 44

Sullivan, Arthur, 159, 160, 196

Svenningsen, Sigrun, 161, 196

Tak! i lige maade! (revue), 98, 192

Taxi Driver (1976), 140

Theatre Moderne, 61, 67-69, 73, 77-78, 79, 80-83, 86-94, 97-98, 100-105, 134-135, 137, 140, 142, 145-147, 163, 164, 166, 172, 175, 177, 188

Thanks! Same to You (revue), see *Tak! I lige maade!*

This and That (revue), see *Dit og dat*

Thorne, William, 91, 92

Tillie's Punctured Romance (1914), 122

Til sæters (play), see *To the Mountain Pastures*

Tivoli Theater, 60-64, 69, 190

To the Mountain Pastures (play), 34, 170, 188

Toje, Ebba, 150, 151, 195

Uten en traad (revue), 164-166, 171, 183, 196

Várnay, Alexander, 66, 103

Veiller, Bayard, 62

Verne, Jules, 147, 161
Victoria (Queen, 1819-1901),
  110
Victorian era (period), 110
Wagner, Richard, 58, 104
Wesenlund, Rolv, 180-183
Whipple, George, 173
White Tie Peter (revue), see
  Galla Petter
Wildenvey, Herman, 62
Wilhelm II (German Emperor),
  94, 145-146

Wingar, Ragnvald, 75, 107, 115,
  158, 194, 195, 196
Winter, Wilhelm, 50
Without a Thread (revue), see
  Uten en traad
Woman at Room 23, The, (play),
  104-107, 109, 121, 194
*Woman You Threw Right in My
  Head, The* (revue), see
  *Kvinden du gav mig midt i
  planeten*
Zerlett, Hans H., 161

Lightning Source UK Ltd.
Milton Keynes UK
UKHW010901080223
416610UK00013B/921